Adobes in the Sun

ADOBES IN THE SUN

Portraits of a Tranquil Era

PHOTOGRAPHS BY MORLEY BAER

Text by Augusta Fink

with Amelie Elkinton

 CHRONICLE BOOKS SAN FRANCISCO

". . . the best house is always a frame for living, never the living itself. The people must supply the living."

One afternoon, in the brilliant California sunshine, William Wilson Wurster, architect,
said these few words on the subject of residential design. It is to him, with deep affectionate regard
for his professional stature and his indefatigable personal spirit, that this book is dedicated.

Many people contributed generously to the research data on
which this book is based. But only through the collaboration of
Amelie Elkinton was it possible to assemble the material in
depth for the major portion of the text. Through extensive and
painstaking work in primary sources, she provided accurate and
in many instances original, factual information on the adobes of
the Monterey area. She also supplied the data about the families
whose lives form the foundation of the story material. An
additional debt is due her for participation in preparing the
picture captions and for editing the manuscript.

Printed in the United States of America

Library of Congress Catalog Card No. 72-85173

Designed by Adrian Wilson, San Francisco

Preface

The photographs in this book have been made with love, love for a place and love for a kind of work. I can no longer imagine life without Monterey. Nor can I think of living without photography. A great part of each is in this book.

Circumstances started this book for me one morning some years ago when I drove into Monterey on an errand. For two days and two nights before, it had stormed without let-up. Everything on the coast was soaked, and, for once, I actually enjoyed getting away from our saddle above the beach. I sped past the familiar peaks of the coastal range, across Granite, Malpaso, and Wildcat canyons, through the valley artichokes, up the long hill and down again into the melee of Alvarado Street.

The car sputtered damply as I parked across the small downtown plaza from the Cooper-Molera house. My eyes glanced at the building briefly as I pulled open the rear trunk to check my film case. There were my main pieces of equipment, all of them afloat or in soggy disarray. What good had it done to park the car on the east side of the house so that it would be out of the worst of the storm?

Annoyed and muttering, I pulled each article out and lined them all out on the sidewalk to dry in the sunshine. Then I stood by impatiently. What in the world does one do while waiting for camera equipment to dry on a six-foot patch of Monterey sidewalk?

The impatience moved my eyes back to the Cooper-Molera house, beaming back at me in the morning sunlight. Squinting against the reflected brilliance, I studied that house—its simple, closed-up facade, one plain street-side door flanked by two ordinary windows broadened with open shutters, the high garden wall with its unused carriage gate, and above it all, the balcony running above the sidewalk, then turning quickly to disappear into the inner garden. The house, despite its position on one of the town's main intersections, spoke of dignity, of a self-reliant and introspective people, of a family finding in its home a refuge from the raucous activity of early Monterey.

Beyond the house, I had a glimpse of the huge Molera barns, and across the street was the architecturally more classic Casa Amesti. At the end of the block, I could make out the First Federal Court (which Augusta Fink was to find had been misnamed all these years), and around the corner, barely out of sight, were the Stokes, Gutiérrez, Larkin, and Serrano adobes. Here, close at hand, was the story of Monterey and the origins of the West Coast in its earliest houses. Most of them were built out of the very soil on which they stood. Some were refined and renewed by timber shipped around the horn from New England or by redwood felled right in the coastal forests of the Sur. The buildings were Spanish, yet they reflected the New World and even New England in their natural unobtrusiveness and their simplicity of design. They were monuments of a sort, but they were still living, most of them as today's homes for today's people.

I was suddenly struck with the compelling images of these houses. I started seeing them not as an occasional visitor taking a casual look but as a professional photographer. I had spent the last twenty years pointing my camera at contemporary architecture. That camera now lay in the midst of a slowly drying puddle. Yet I could not wait. I had to put those venerable homes on film. In an almost grand gesture, I pulled the still-soggy camera off the pavement, placed it on its big wooden tripod, and went to work. It was to be the first exposure of many which I began to call the Monterey Historical Series. MHS was to become a special drawer in the file, and, later, with practical guidance, the series was to be compressed and synthesized, almost drawn and quartered. At last, in a concerted effort with many others, the collection was to become "the adobe book".

And what lies behind this need to record the town and its buildings, to photograph a clean, white chimney or a simple, laced window pane? What has sparked my love of photography and of Monterey? Perhaps 1946, when the world began again (out of uniform and on the coast of California, at last!), would be a reasonable starting point in time.

There were picnics at Point Lobos with a small, gentle man who carried a big camera. He never taught, and he never pointed, and those around him simply absorbed. What he was to say in quiet, uncomplicated ways, and what he had already photographed of his western world was to be an incalculable legacy. Edward Weston not only planted the seed but nurtured much of the ground from which many other photographers were to grow. The clear, direct view, with and without the camera, seemed to begin here. Without ever intending to, he ennobled not only the act of photographing but that of living. And he made California, particularly the natural and man-made forms of the Monterey coast, a world to see and instantly to love.

There was also a young lady who was carrying a child inside of her when we first met in the late '40s. Her husband had just shed his army sergeant's uniform, and they had returned to Monterey to take up a life torn apart five years earlier. She said she wanted her children to know and love the heritage of Monterey as she and her family had known it. She spoke often of the earliest houses with the oldest gardens, and she reminded me "to go around in back to see where things are still growing." And although her husband was to walk down Alvarado Street one day and be spat upon, Mariko Sumida remained in this town she loved and spoke with more consideration and knowledge of the Monterey adobes and their gardens than most of their own inhabitants.

There was one afternoon at Tor House. I had been asked by a magazine to make a photograph of Robinson Jeffers, that tall, gray eminence responsible for *Medea.* As I did so, he seemed aloof, detached (I never knew until much later how ill he was). But seeing him in the mirror of my Graflex made me want to go back to the words I had first read with little understanding years before. Now, *Roan Stallion, Tamar, The Women at Point Sur,* and *Thurso's Landing* suddenly took on meaning. I now knew the places and I sensed the spirit and force with which Jeffers summoned the coastlands. The words remained with me, and I remained in Monterey.

There were others, many others. The need to photograph is my own, but the motivations and the subject matter have come through many different people whose words and acts I cherish. They have brought me to "the adobe book" with what I can hope is a clear eye, an understanding of the material, and a recognition of what light can do with it.

Morley Baer
Monterey, August 1972

Contents

Adobe mud, the source of adobe brick

The Adobe Way of Life

Made of the earth and oriented to the sun, adobe architecture represents a unique aspect of the California heritage. Designed to meet the straightforward needs of a simple people, it also symbolizes a way of life which reflects the best in the American dream. Built of mud bricks, cemented by the rays of the sun, the unadorned abodes of another era stand today as an affirmation of the beauty that abides in man's uncomplicated interaction with the planet he inhabits.

Soldiers and padres from Spain first brought the ancient art of adobe construction to Mexico and then to California. Here the formula, handed down through the ages from Egyptian and Babylonian times, was adapted to the conditions of soil and temperature found in a new land. It was an inexact formula, learned by word of mouth and example and passed from one generation to the next.

The customary procedure was to begin by digging a large basin in the ground, about twenty feet in diameter and two feet deep. Into this was put soil and water, mixed with whatever "binders" were available at the site. These might be reeds from a neighboring stream, weeds from a nearby field, or shells from the beach. Even birds' nests and refuse were used. When the mixture was of a thick, soupy consistency, it was poured into molds and dried in the sun. Out of the resulting adobe bricks, generally 11 by 22 inches in size, were built the massive three-foot deep walls that characterize adobe construction.

The method was taught by the padres to Indian converts to Catholicism, from whose labor emerged the mission structures patterned after models from Spain. Then, with the coming of the first families to California, with their yearning for a hearth more permanent than one fashioned of poles and twigs, the unique provincial architectural form known as California Colonial came into being. The first dwellings, often erected by the settlers themselves, were exceedingly primitive. They consisted of one room, a tule roof and dirt floor, and openings for windows and door protected from the elements by rawhide hangings fastened to the crude frames. There were no furnishings, except for a mat spread on a slightly elevated portion of the earthen floor and possibly a few cushions.

The site of the house was carefully selected. All-important was the proximity of a stream or a spring for fresh water. Another consideration was the elevation and openness of the terrain: if possible, a level, treeless spot on high ground was chosen, which would afford protection from water erosion of the mud walls and allow an early alert to Indian attack. Almost always the dwelling was placed crosswise to the points of the compass so that the maximum amount of cherished sunlight would be lured inside.

By the beginning of the 19th century, adobe dwellings were clustered in newly founded pueblos as well as in the areas adjoining presidios. They were larger but still one-story, rectangular in shape, and typically had three rooms opening one into another, with a small separate structure or lean-to for a kitchen. The flooring was the earth, tamped to a smooth surface and hardened by watering. Whitewash covered the mud-plastered adobe walls, and roughhewn beams supported the tule roof fastened with leather thongs. A few simple pieces of furniture now appeared in the homes of the middle-class—a crude table, a couple of benches, and a bed made of a wood frame to which were laced rawhide strips.

Gradually a few refinements in building construction evolved. Windows were secured against intruders by wooden poles set a few inches apart in the small openings, and tiles began to replace tule as a roofing material. Shaped on wooden molds, the tiles were somewhat larger than the Spanish models after which they were patterned. Many were sixteen inches across the big end. To accept the legend that these were molded over shapely thighs requires belief that some Indian maids were Amazons.

The opening of the port of Monterey to foreign trade, in 1822, presaged significant changes in the primitive design of the earliest adobes. Soon trading vessels from all of the world, many from New England, anchored in the great bay. Aboard were workmen who brought new carpentry skills to the formerly isolated province of California, and small innovations were introduced into standard adobe construction. Then, in 1833, the man who was to pioneer a different concept of adobe design, Thomas Oliver Larkin, arrived in Monterey.

Utilizing the skilled labor of Scotch and Irish immigrants from Yankee and British ships, Larkin began construction of his home in 1835. Though built of adobe brick, a strong redwood frame made possible an upper story, as well as more freedom in the placement of windows. The design rested primarily on the building traditions of New England, but also incorporated some elements from the Southern plantation. From the Eastern American colonial pattern came the floor plan, interior staircase, and hipped roof covered with shingles. But the verandas, built to protect the walls from water erosion, were reminiscent of the Southern plantation. All the luxuries still scarcely known in the province were included—two fireplaces, plank flooring, wallpaper, milled doors, and small-paneled double-sash glass windows. The Larkin house, which took three years to build, established a new style of architecture—the Monterey Colonial.

In the ensuing decade, great prosperity came to California through the hide and tallow trade, and Monterey was the center of life for the northern portion of the province. Wealthy merchants and rancheros emulated the Larkin style of adobe architecture, both in building new houses and in enlarging existing structures. With increased affluence also came a demand for the amenities of the outside world. Canny captains of commercial vessels added home furnishings to their bulging cargoes. Many pieces were imported from the Orient and Peru—marble-topped and inlaid tables, handsome bureaus, rosewood desks, rattan chairs, and large mirrors. Chinese tableware became popular with families who could afford it, and hardly a home of any means was without at least one brightly painted, leather-covered camphorwood chest in which to keep clothing and linens. Adobe construction did not provide for closets.

Showpiece of the house was the bed. Enormous in size, its frame might be rawhide stretched on wood or an elegant four-poster, but invariably it was covered with snowy, lace-fringed sheets, piles of pillows cased in silken material, and an elaborately decorated coverlet. And all this atop a mattress made of corn shucks!

The Stevenson House, rear courtyard

In 1843, the first pianos were brought to California, three in number. And a year later, Thomas Larkin ordered a complete set of American furniture for his home. Among the items listed were two pairs of sofas (one pair of which could be converted into beds) a pair each of large dining tables and of heavy round tables, a pair of washstands, and four large "National" pictures with handsome frames. The wealthy who were so inclined could now copy the New England style of decor as well as architecture. But for families of modest means, home furnishings were still confined to a couple of beds, a table, and a few chairs. And for everyone the life-style remained simple and related to the outdoors.

All adobe dwellings had an adjoining patio or walled-in area where much family living took place. Both patios and verandas usually faced south to soak up the sun. Hospitality was the credo of the early Californians, and the layout of their homes reflected their outgoing temperament. A large *sala*, sometimes on the second floor, provided space for entertaining. In the dining room was a long table that could seat many guests. And no traveller was ever turned away without at least the courtesy of a cool drink. For this refreshment, there stood in readiness on a sideboard a decanter of brandy or wine, a pitcher of fresh water, and a bowl of sugar. The customary beverage was compounded of two-thirds water, one-third spirits and a little sweetening.

Separate adobe kitchens were the rule. These had earthen floors and were equipped with only a plain wooden table. Garlic and other seasonings hung from the rafters in strings or bunches. As there were no sinks, water was brought in from a barrel that stood at the door and was replenished from a stream or well. When preparing vegetables, the housewife or Indian servant used two large pans of water, one for cleaning

and the other for keeping the food until it was time for it to be cooked. There were three arrangements for cooking and baking. Outside the kitchen was a big, cone-shaped bake oven as well as a broiling pit dug in the ground. Over the latter, meat was suspended on long spits above the hot coals and hand-turned until it was done. Vegetables, beans, and tortillas were cooked on *hornillas*—little ovens consisting of two layers of stone, about eight inches high and two feet long, placed about fourteen inches apart, over which an iron plate was laid. This plate, called a *comal*, served the same purpose as the top of a stove.

Not only were indoor toilet facilities nonexistent, but bathing also took place outdoors. Ranch families simply swam in a nearby stream. Those who lived in town had an open shed built around the well on their property, where they stripped and used buckets of water for their lavations. In winter, a sponge bath was possible from a tub of water in the kitchen.

Washday was the occasion for an excursion. Clothes were piled in a *carreta*, and the whole family journeyed to the nearest rivulet of running water. There the women kneeled over boards three feet long, placed on the bank, and rubbed away the dirt. It was an all-day procedure, and women who had Indian servants to do the back-breaking manual labor could enjoy a leisurely visit with their friends.

Housekeeping in an adobe was uncomplicated. Floors were swept with a broom, which in many homes was simply a bundle of rushes tied tightly together. Before the advent of plank flooring, a daily sprinkling of water kept down the dust and hardened the surface. Later a plain matting was used as carpeting. To control dust sifting down through the boards of the open ceilings, canvas or cotton cloth was stretched below the rafters and tacked to nailing strips around the top of the walls. Every spring a coat of whitewash was applied to both the exterior and interior of the house. Easily prepared by mixing lime and a little salt in a bucket of water, the whitewash protected the adobe material and served as a deodorant and disinfectant as well. Often a delicate coloring was added to the white. The soft pinks, blues, and greens were pleasing and still did not darken the rooms.

Lighting was a problem. The small barred windows let in little sunlight—another reason for spending as much time as possible outdoors. Great quantities of candles were used, and later whale-oil lamps came into vogue. Pine flares illuminated preparation of the evening meal in the patio and lighted the way to the outbuildings.

Nostalgia for the life-style of early California must include an understanding of the lack of its comforts—the amenities taken for granted today. Its appeal stems from a spiritual response to a time when man was in intimate touch with his surroundings. Both his architecture and his way of life were uncluttered by material things. Each task was performed without haste or tension, and involved a feeling for the essence of the object in hand. Out of the earth came the sustenance of life, and its fruits were treated with respect. What if women spent three hours grinding corn for a single family meal? It was a part of the seamless web of their days, in which every activity had an equal place. Each moment was savored to its fullest, whether at work or play, and the clean, uncomplicated architecture of the adobe symbolizes the simplicity of an era more meaningful than that of contemporary existence.

In this book are examples of the many forms in which the secular adobe architecture of Northern California was expressed. Built over the fifty-year period beginning in 1817, these adobes range in size from the one-room José de Jesús

Kitchen in Stevenson House as it may have looked during the Girardin occupancy, second half of the nineteenth century.

The Sánchez Adobe

Vallejo adobe in Alameda County to the huge, fortress-like home of General Vallejo in the Petaluma area of Sonoma. They include the unpretentious dwellings of pioneer settlers, like that of José Joaquín Soto, and the spacious townhouses of the Amestis and the Ábregos. Reflecting the ranchero period are the commodious homes of Francisco Sánchez and Vicente Martinez, as well as such snug, pastoral abodes as the home of the Tresconys. In addition to private dwellings, government buildings and commercial structures are represented, with the Cooper-Molera complex epitomizing an important aspect of town life in early Monterey.

All of the adobes are still standing, their beautifully proportioned rooms seeming to radiate a welcome to all who enter their massive walls. Mellowed by the years, the stark, white facades are unspoiled by ornamentation. The secluded courtyards and graceful balconies conjure the carefree hours of a more tranquil era. From the traditions of Spain and New England, expressed through the building materials of California, an architectural heritage of deeply moving significance has been preserved for future generations.

Adobes in the Sun

East porch of the Ábrego house.

Casa Ábrego

It was a proud day for the twenty-three-year-old José Ábrego when he brought his lovely bride, María Joséfa Estrada, to the charming adobe he had prepared for her. Only two years earlier, in 1834, he had arrived in Monterey with a large group of colonists lured by promises of land which did not materialize. Some of the *pobladores* had returned to Mexico, but Ábrego prudently invested his small capital and successfully pursued his career as hatter and merchant. On his wedding day, he owned a 100-foot-square lot on which stood a thriving mercantile establishment as well as the delightful new home.

Marriage to María Joséfa made him a member of several influential families – the Estradas, of course, and the Vallejos, Lugos, and Alvarados as well. Doña Joséfa's half-brother was the charismatic Juan Bautista Alvarado, newly elected governor of California. He and Joséfa had grown up together in Monterey in the Vallejo adobe, home of their beloved "*nana* Antonia". The youthful governor, whom Joséfa was said to idolize, was a frequent guest at the Casa Ábrego, as was Joséfa's uncle, the dashing General Mariano Vallejo. *Tio* Mariano's visits were always a gala event. Adored by everyone, he insisted on kissing everything feminine, from six to sixty, amid peals of laughter and fun.

As might be expected, José Ábrego prospered rather quickly. He was awarded the contract for construction of *El Cuartel,* a two-story government building erected by Governor Alvarado. He was also one of the grantees for the Rancho Punta de Pinos.

Restored south end of building.

As Don José became ever more affluent, his *casa* expanded until it covered almost a square block, with the merchandise store moved to the corner of present-day Pearl Street. Inside the expanded adobe, there was now a spacious ballroom and a large dining room in which fourteen guests could be seated comfortably around the long rosewood table. The luxuriously furnished *sala* was graced by one of the three pianos in all of California. Delegates to the Constitutional Convention enjoyed many evenings of relaxation dancing the quadrille and the polka to its music. At the rear of the house, glowing masses of roses and fuchsia grew in the walled-in garden, and a stately magnolia tree perfumed the air with the sharp, sweet fragrance of its blossoms. In springtime, the fruit orchard enclosed in a second patio added clouds of vibrant color above the white adobe walls.

Don José remained a highly respected and exceedingly popular member of the Monterey community up to his death in 1878, at the age of sixty-five. Doña Joséfa survived him by almost twenty years, remaining at the Casa Ábrego until her death in 1897. One grandson recorded fond memories of her sitting before the fireplace in her high-ceilinged bedroom, singing a lilting lullaby to him.

Shortly after Doña Joséfa's death, the house was sold and allowed to deteriorate. By 1917, only a small portion of the once vast *casa* remained, and this was carefully restored to preserve much of its original charm. The building is now the headquarters of the Casa Ábrego Club, which comprises a group of women dedicated to conservation of the Monterey heritage.

Balustrade at main entry door.

Casa Alvarado

The smaller of Governor Juan Bautista Alvarado's two town-houses in Monterey was a modest three-room adobe, roofed with tule, that stood not far from his grandmother Antonia Vallejo's home. Probably built in the early 1830s, the Casa Alvarado was typical of the architecture of its time. Fashioned of sun-dried earthen bricks, it had walls three-feet thick and rafters fastened by rawhide and wooden pegs. Simple shuttered openings hung with cloth or leather served as windows.

From the deed records of adjoining properties, one may deduce that the small *casa* was occupied for several years by a beautiful young woman with whom Alvarado maintained a liason. She was Raimunda Castillo, daughter of the town bloodletter. Apparently devoted to Alvarado, she bore him three children.

By 1839, the thirty-year-old governor who found his office fraught with problems, was drinking heavily and in poor health. Possibly to assume the mantle of respectability, he married Martina Castro, member of two prominent Northern California families. Not long after his marriage, the world-weary Alvarado retired to the country, purchasing the Rancho El Alisal in the Salinas Valley. In 1842, he sold the little *casa* in Monterey to Manuel Dutra for 100 silver dollars. His state of mind is revealed by his memoirs: "I, who had the misfortune to become a public man, can assert that politics is the most ungrateful career that a man can follow, and that which brings the most unhappiness."

Casa Alvarado facing Dutra Street.

Meanwhile, the Casa Alvarado's former occupant, Raimunda Castillo, had a brighter outlook. She found both happiness and security in 1844, when she became the wife of a wealthy landowner, Mariano de Jesús Soberanes, and lived out her days on the sunny Rancho Los Ojitos near the Mission San Antonio.

Soon after the American annexation of California, hard times hit Monterey, and, more than once, Manuel Dutra was forced to mortgage his property at interest rates of as much as five percent per month! But the Dutras managed to retain their home and resided there for many years, maintaining a store at one end of the building. Eventually, the house became the property of a daughter, Joséfa Dutra Kinlock, and in 1946 it was sold by her heirs. Now beautifully restored, the Casa Alvarado, a private residence, is a fine example of early adobe design.

Casa Amesti

Balcony of Casa Amesti through the garden.

Born in the Basque seaport town of San Sebastian, José Amesti came to Monterey via Mexico in 1821 and established himself as a merchant. Soon he was attracted to sixteen-year-old Prudenciana Vallejo, daughter of the old pioneer soldier Ignacio Vicente Vallejo. Though Don José was twice her age, the courtly, well-educated and enterprising Spaniard easily won the young girl's heart and the approval of her father. The marriage was solemnized in 1822. Hardship and heartache awaited the young bride.

The couple left immediately for the isolated Corralitos area near Santa Cruz, where Amesti was petitioning for a land grant. Inadequately attended at the birth of her first child, she almost died and for months was unable to walk. Her spine was permanently crippled. Added to the burden of ill health was her discovery that her husband had a fiery temper and "could be most cruel."

After twelve lonely and difficult years, Prudenciana returned with her husband and three daughters to live in Monterey in a newly built one-story adobe, the Casa Amesti. Close by, in a small adobe on present-day Pierce Street, lived her mother, María Antonia Vallejo. Other family members resided a short walk away. It was the beginning of a time of comparative happiness for the frail young gentlewoman.

Don José, whose wealth and prestige greatly increased, gradually transformed the Casa Amesti into a showplace worthy of his position. By 1853, when the second story and

Modern garden on southwest side of building.

Foot scraper and oak bench.

Adobe brick wall with tile capping.

Old courtyard door of Monterey pine.

southern portion of the house had been added, the fine home was complete. Guests were received in the grand upstairs *sala,* where the highly polished floor was said to be "greatly prized for dancing because of its springiness." Elegant dinner parties were held around a magnificent dining room table with 36 matching chairs. Long, graceful balconies made a perfect setting for an afternoon visit over a cup of chocolate. And many a fiesta was held in the large walled-in garden, where the cooking and other household activities were performed in small separate buildings.

During these years, Doña Prudenciana, despite her exacting duties as hostess and a worsened physical condition, devoted herself to those in the community who were in need. She survived her husband by twenty-eight years, and after his death, in 1855, she made the *casa* a center for her religious and charitable activities. She took food to the poor and personally prepared the destitute for burial. Greatly loved and respected, she lived in the Casa Amesti until her death at the age of seventy-eight.

The Casa Amesti remained in the possession of the family until about 1913. Then, according to some recollections, the *casa* became a boarding-house, run by a flower-fancying Frenchwoman whose plants occupied the sidewalk and part of the street. In 1918, the Casa Amesti was purchased by Mr. and Mrs. Felton Elkins, who restored it as their residence. Frances Elkins, a noted interior decorator, furnished the adobe with beautiful period pieces and bequeathed it to the National Trust for Historic Preservation. Today, maintained by the Old Capital Club, the Casa Amesti stands as a superb example of Monterey Colonial architecture.

Newel-post on upstairs balustrade.

Framing of double doorway illustrates fine
workmanship representative of New England
carpentry.

Opening between dining room and *sala.*
Furnishings do not reflect adobe period.

Casa Bonifacio

Originally located at the present-day intersection of Alvarado Street and Bonifacio Place in Monterey, the adobe that belonged to the Bonifacios is surrounded by the aura of two romantic love stories. Through an earlier owner, José María Castanares, it is also associated with one of early Monterey's more notorious scandals.

Clerk and son-in-law of the administrator of customs, Castanares was involved in an illicit love affair with the wife of another town official. When they were found out, the woman testified that when she had tried to resist his advances, because of friendship for his spouse, the rash young man had threatened to remove that "obstacle to their felicity by the use of poison." Banished for his behavior, Castanares sold the adobe in the mid-1830s and left for Mexico.

The *casa* became Casa Bonifacio when Doña Carmen Pinto de Bonifacio bought the two-story, four-room house. She was the widow of an immigrant Italian who had come to Monterey as a stevedore. One of her three children was María Ygnacia, who, at the time of the American occupation, was a lovely, velvet-eyed fifteen. Lieutenant William Tecumseh Sherman, then a young officer stationed in Monterey, was attracted to the charming girl. Unfortunately, he was already betrothed to the daughter of a prominent Eastern family.

Many believe that a cloth-of-gold rose vine that grew in the adobe's walled-in garden was planted from a blossom brought to María Ygnacia by Sherman before his departure. Others discredit this story—the legend of the Sherman Rose—saying that María actually had another admirer, a handsome *Californio* whom she really loved, but that her mother refused to approve the marriage. One fact is certain; Señorita Bonifacio remained a spinster, living a lonely existence in the sheltered adobe. In her upstairs bedroom was a leather-covered chest in which she stored the finery reminiscent of bygone days: wasp-waisted dresses of crimson velvet and stiff brocade, embroidered mittens, and tiny slippers for dancing feet.

The delicate lace work in which Señorita Bonifacio was highly skilled helped to support her and her aging mother. They also rented out rooms in the Casa Bonifacio, an enterprise that led to the second romantic tale associated with the house. In 1879, Robert Louis Stevenson's beloved Fanny Osbourne occupied a wing of the house. Once again romance flourished amidst the fragrant garden of the golden roses, as Stevenson came every afternoon to read his stories aloud to Fanny. Perhaps the presence of lovers brightened María Ygnacia's life a little.

After her mother died in 1882, María Ygnacia lived out her days alone in the large home, until her own death came in 1916, at the age of eighty-three. In accord with her wishes, those possessions still remaining in the leather chest were buried with her. They included a fine silk dress, some undergarments, a military sword, and a packet of letters tied with a ribbon. The letters were from Sherman.

After Señorita Bonifacio's death, the Casa Bonifacio was sold and the adobe dismantled. It was then reconstructed on the mesa, behind the old Royal Presidio Chapel, for the artist Percy Gray. There it stands today, with part of the old golden rose vine growing over the trellis at the front door.

Contemporary interpretation of adobe life.

Casa Boronda, Carmel Valley

José Manuel Boronda, son of the schoolmaster, came to live in the Carmel Valley in 1840. With him was his wife, Juana, and their large brood of children. The Rancho Los Laureles had been granted jointly to Boronda and to Vicente Blas Martinez, but Don José was the one who chose to make his home there. His adobe, which was nestled in laurel trees near the Carmel River, consisted of three rooms with dirt floors, crudely raftered ceilings and a thatched roof. He and his eldest son, Juan de Mata, had prepared the dwelling for occupancy by adding to a building that had once housed an Indian family.

The young Borondas worked hard, gradually enlarging their small herd of cattle and planting grain. Before long, Doña Juana was making great round mounds of yellow cheese from the rich milk that became plentiful. There were gay times, too. Friends and relatives frequently took the long trek from Monterey and the Salinas Valley for fiestas. A delicacy, often prepared for such occasions, was a bull's head wrapped in wet sacking and slowly steamed in a pit of glowing coals. In front of the adobe was a fenced arena in which bull and bear fights were held for the enjoyment of the guests. The bears used in the sport had sometimes been captured by the young Juan de Mata, who was famous in the area for stalking the beasts alone, and in the dead of night, when they came to lick salt along the marshes near the beach.

In 1851, the Borondas bought out Martinez's half interest for eight horses, one mare, and six cows, becoming then the

Morning sun lights red brick and wide plank flooring of patio doorway.

Thick walls, wide plank floor, and white open rafters typify adobe interior.

sole owners of more than 6,000 acres of fertile valley land. But unfortunately for them, the heyday of the rancheros was drawing to a close. By the end of the next decade, the rancho was acquired by Nathan Spaulding of San Francisco, who in turn sold it to the Pacific Improvement Company, the financial representative of the West Coast's financial Big Four— Crocker, Stanford, Huntington and Hopkins.

Soon, a large dairy operation was centered in the Boronda adobe. Huge vats and presses were installed in the *casa* to manufacture great quantities of the golden cheese which had once been made by Doña Juana. The process was the same, only larger in volume. Doña Juana had used simply a single keg, with a heavy board across the top pressed down by a jack. Some say that is how the cheese came to be called Monterey Jack.

After the Pacific Improvement Company disposed of the property, the Casa Boronda fell into disrepair. For years it stood, with its crumbling walls and fallen roof-beam, as a poignant reminder of the days of the dons. At last, in the 1940s, it came into the possession of someone who appreciated its unique value, and the neglected building was carefully restored. A protective coat of plaster was applied outside the three-foot thick walls, plank flooring was laid down with hand-made pegs, and the roof was repaired with antique tiles. Modern conveniences were unobtrusively installed. Finally, the Casa Boronda was once again a private residence, filled with life and laughter, and so it stands today.

Massive adobe wall rises to ridgepole.

Simplicity of doorway contrasts with later decorative doorlatch.

Casa Boronda, Monterey

A great favorite of Father Serra, Manuel Boronda was a retired corporal who had spent twenty years throughout Alta California utilizing his skills as a carpenter in the service of the padres. At the San Francisco presidio, he had also acted as schoolmaster, and he resumed this occupation in the late 1790s when he resettled in Monterey with his young wife Gertrudis. There were no dwellings outside the protection of the presidio walls at that time, so for two decades, the Borondas lived in one of the rude structures that lined the garrison quadrangle. Then, in 1817, Manuel requested a parcel of land back of the presidio chapel and joined the half-dozen hardy souls who were already building their homes on the mesa. The Boronda site was on a ridge, between two canyons, only a short walking distance from the church.

The Casa Boronda was a simple adobe, consisting of a small center room with two slightly larger ones on either side. Following the gentle slope of the hill on which it was built, the level of the house was fifteen inches lower at its northern end. Rough-hewn beams supported a tule roof fastened with leather thongs. Rawhide coverings hung over the openings that served as windows and door. Cooking was done outdoors in a cone-shaped bake oven, and a lean-to provided shelter for the preparation of food.

Soon one of the rooms was outfitted for a school. The schoolboys sat on long wooden benches facing Don Manuel, who was seated in a straight-back chair with rawhide bottom,

Modern planting screens slope of hundred and fifty year old adobe.

his feet resting on a bear rug. On the table in front of him were textbooks bound in sheepskin and a stack of coarse cartridge paper so scarce that each boy was allotted no more than two pieces a day and was severely reprimanded if he spoiled a sheet. Subjects taught included religion, reading, arithmetic, singing, elocution and deportment.

Less than a year after the Boronda adobe was completed, Monterey was attacked by Hippolyte Bouchard and his privateers, who looted and burned buildings throughout the small settlement. In a squeaking, wooden-wheeled *carreta,* Doña Gertrudis was among the women who fled with their families to the safety of the Salinas Valley. Situated in its exposed location, the home of the Borondas was undoubtedly one of the dwellings to be badly damaged. The heartbreaking incident was but one of many trials endured by early residents.

Though Manuel Boronda had several sons, his youngest daughter, the petite and pious Petra, eventually inherited the adobe. At the tender age of thirteen, she had married George Allen, an Englishman and Quaker who had been baptized into the Catholic Church, and it was he who installed wooden floors in the house, replaced the thatched roof with tile, and added other modest comforts to lighten the workload of his womenfolk. Subsequently, the large, bustling families of five generations were raised in the Boronda adobe. Today, Casa Boronda still stands as a private dwelling, at the end of Boronda Lane off Fremont Street.

The Castro Adobe

Near the eastern boundary of the Rancho San Andrés, in present-day Santa Cruz County, is a beautiful two-story adobe which once belonged to descendants of Joaquín Ysidro Castro. Founder of one of California's foremost families, Joaquín Ysidro came to Monterey, in 1776, as one of the de Anza colonists, with his wife and eight children, including the six-year-old José Joaquín. The family first settled at the newly established presidio of San Francisco, and later were among the pioneers who founded the pueblo of San Jose. In 1787, at the age of seventeen, José Joaquín left home to become a soldier and was stationed at the Monterey presidio. Four years later, he married María Antonia Amador. When the village of Branciforte (Santa Cruz) was established in 1797, he was transferred there with his wife and two small children. By 1823, José Joaquín's family had increased to eleven sons and daughters. To provide a more secure future for them, he requested a piece of land on which he could herd cattle and establish a permanent homestead. He was given a provisional grant to the Rancho San Andrés, which was later confirmed. The rancho, as eventually patented, comprised 8911 acres.

Though Castro erected two houses and a corral on the Rancho San Andrés, he continued to live in Santa Cruz. Then, in 1828, Doña María Antonia died. A widower who had only two minor children still living at home, he found comfort in the charms of the seventeen-year-old Rosaria Briones. They were married in 1830, and for his bride Castro built another

Late afternoon sun laces through wisteria and orange trees. Note the tie-bolt above excessively low doorway.

Outside staircase is typical of early adobes.

adobe on a hill overlooking the beautiful Pajaro Valley, in the eastern portion of the Rancho San Andrés.

It is possible that this adobe was only the small, one-story structure that now forms the northeast wing of the present-day house for, among other indications, the timbers of the main building are mill-sawn, and the first sawmill in the area did not open until 1842. Some say that the dwelling was the idyllic abode of the old soldier and his young wife until his death, at the age of sixty-eight, in 1838. The widow, Dona Rosaria, was left with three little children, and not long after remarried. According to one source, she continued to live in the San Andrés adobe, sharing it with two of José Joaquín's sons by his first marriage, whom she subsequently sued over distribution of the property.

At this point, the story becomes somewhat obscure; Juan José Castro, second youngest son of Don José Joaquín's first marriage, did inherit the portion of the Rancho San Andrés on which Doña Rosaria's adobe stood. Census records show that he and his family resided on the rancho as well as in the town of Santa Cruz. It can only be surmised that Juan José Castro won the legal battle with his stepmother, took over the adobe, and enlarged it to the 30 by 100-foot proportions shown in early pictures. In any event, he lost the property in 1874 through a mortgage foreclosure and, by 1915, the once proud house that had boasted a 30 by 50-foot fandango room on its second floor had degenerated in use to a hay barn and storage building. But a few years later, it was restored as a private residence. The collapsing southeast endwall was replaced with concrete and buttresses, and subsequent owners have continued discretely to improve without impairing its original proportions and appearance.

Chamfered posts add touch of refinement.

Missouri workmen were responsible for the
original adobe.

The Chiles Adobe

North of Napa, nestled in a lovely hidden valley, is an adobe built by the intrepid trail-blazer Joseph Ballinger Chiles. A widower who had lost his childhood sweetheart, he had been forced to place his four small children in the care of relatives. Lonely and restive, he sought the release of unknown horizons, and arrived in California in 1841 as one of an expeditionary party that pioneered a route across the Sierras.

Chiles, then thirty-one and in his prime, his towering six-foot-four frame well suited to the arduous tasks of a frontiersman, first saw the valley that was to bear his name in the fall of that year. An experienced farmer, he was instantly captivated by the lush grassy meadows and gently rounded hills. Though he returned temporarily to his home in Missouri, he resolved that this land someday would be his. Early in 1844, he was back in California, having led his own party to the beautiful country he had found, and in November he was granted the 8500-acre Rancho Catacula.

There in the valley of his dreams, he built a log cabin and began construction of a flour mill. By the winter of 1846, the walls of an adobe dwelling had been raised. Arrival of a large wagon train from Missouri provided workers to speed its completion, and soon several families with their children were housed in the three-room structure. Even the cabin and a lean-to back of the adobe were filled to overflowing. Cooking was done in the fireplace, in the north room of the adobe, and evenings were spent in spelling matches or listening to Chiles

Extended eaves were intended to keep the rain off the adobe walls.

play the violin. Quilting bees occupied the women during the rainy season, and these became popular social gatherings for residents from miles around. By the summer of 1847, both a wedding and a birth had taken place in the adobe. It was a real home, alive with warm fellowship, and Chiles was content. He then once again took the long journey east to Missouri—this time to bring his own children, now teenagers, to the place he had established. A year later, in October of 1848, he returned to find the Catacula more beautiful than ever. Purple clusters of grapes shone in the sunlit vineyard, and the thin trunks of young locust trees cast shadows on the walls of the waiting adobe. There were signs of prosperity, too. Sleek cattle grazed on the hills, fat haystacks dotted the landscape, the sheds bulged with corn, and the mill was teeming with activity. Best of all, his pride and joy—the prize-winning black mules he had brought across the plains and mountains in '44 were flourishing. Three attractive daughters soon brought the sound of laughter and young voices to the Chiles adobe. Even after they were married, they spent time on the old homestead. In November, 1851, two births took place in the adobe within three days, with the versatile Chiles acting as midwife. But by 1853, the girls were established in homes of their own, and Chiles was overcome with loneliness.

He departed for Missouri and brought back a bride, seventeen years his junior. Along the trail to California, a son was born—the start of a new family for the jubilant Chiles. Strangely, he felt that the adobe which he had cherished was not suitable for his young wife. He built a commodious dwelling on acreage in what is now Rutherford, and other members of the Chiles family took over the old home. In the 1860s, after a series of financial reverses, he returned briefly to the Catacula with his family. Then, in 1872, he moved to St. Helena, where he lived until his death in 1885.

Descendants of a nephew of Joseph Chiles retained possession of the adobe until 1943. Its present owner has carefully restored the venerable house, which served for over a century as a family dwelling. Today, immaculately preserved, it is used as a weekend and summer home.

The Los Coches Adobe

Situated south of Soledad in the Salinas valley is a two-story adobe and wood building which is well over a hundred years old. Its ancient walls have housed the simple family life of the early rancheros, a bustling hotel and stage coach stop, and in more recent times a rowdy, roadside tavern. But its story begins in 1842, when it was built as a home for María Joséfa Soberanes by her husband, William Brenner Richardson.

Granddaughter of the pioneer soldier, José María Soberanes, who came to California with the Portolá expedition, Joséfa was a member of one of the wealthiest and most distinguished families of the area. She was in her late twenties when she married, in 1839, and her father, the influential Don Feliciano, wished to provide a secure future for his eldest child. Richardson, an emigrant from Maryland whose bright-colored hair caused him to be called "William the Red," was only a lowly tailor. The Soberanes family already owned huge acreage in the Salinas Valley and, in 1841, Don Feliciano persuaded Governor Alvarado to grant the 8794-acre Rancho Los Coches to his daughter. It adjoined the Soledad Mission lands, of which Don Feliciano was administrator, and was not far from his 21,884-acre Rancho San Lorenzo.

For a homesite, Richardson chose a spot overlooking the oak-bordered Salinas River to the east and the towering Santa Lucia Mountains to the west. There he constructed a two-room adobe and planted a row of black locust trees to shade its front. To this modest dwelling came the proud Doña Joséfa

Long corridor with earthen floor is setting for work or relaxation.

with their two-year-old baby girl. The 300 head of cattle, given to her by her father, were pastured on the land, and Richardson worked hard to succeed at his new occupation of ranchero.

Four years later, Captain John C. Fremont camped on the Rancho Los Coches with his troops, helping himself to cattle, horses, and other supplies worth several hundred dollars. It was a loss the Richardsons could ill afford. But a new source of income was devised by the resourceful daughter of the Soberanes. She transformed her home into a flourishing stage stop. A wooden second story addition was built on the adobe, and the San Juan-Soledad stage brought a lively trade. Later the place became popular as an inn for passengers of the Bixby Overland line en route from San Francisco to Los Angeles.

Still the Richardsons ran into severe financial problems. Costly litigation in the courts, required to defend title to their land after American occupation, drained the family funds. Then the advent of the 1860's brought a killing drought. Cattle dropped by the thousands. All rancheros were in trouble, and the Richardsons became heavily indebted to a merchant in Monterey. Doña Joséfa was forced to mortgage the property her father had obtained for her. The $1800 she borrowed came at 2% per month, with interest to be compounded four times a year.

In 1865, the Rancho Los Coches was acquired by David Jacks in a sheriff's sale. Though the Richardsons no longer owned the property, the family continued to live in the old adobe for many years. As late as the 1890's, a nephew of Doña Joséfa was residing there and recorded memories of cascaron balls and lavish dinner parties held on the premises. Then, after the turn of the century, old-timers recall the house being used as a hotel and saloon—a "real hot spot" to which people came from miles around for a rousing good time.

Ninety-three years after David Jacks acquired Los Coches, his daughter, Miss Margaret Jacks, donated the adobe and ten surrounding acres to the state. Today a small, wayside park adjoins the building, and the stately row of locust trees still stands in front of its porch. The aura of a bygone era clings to the weatherbeaten house, gently mellowed by the years, and its setting conjures images of the rich history it has known. A movement, spear-headed by a granddaughter of the Richardsons, is underway to restore the venerable adobe, now a State Historical Monument, as a museum.

Aged black locusts were planted to provide
protection from valley wind and sun.

Cantilevered veranda, added in 1850, dominates eastern facade. Paneled shutters add unusual detail to older first floor.

The Cooper-Molera Adobes

At the south end of Alvarado Street in Monterey stands a group of structures known as the old Cooper place. For more than a century, this large complex of walled-in adobes has represented the life-style of old Monterey, with its combination of private dwellings and business establishments. The oldest building in the group, located midway along Polk Street, was a storehouse constructed in 1826 by Captain John Rogers Cooper.

Born on Alderney Island, off the coast of Britain, Cooper came to Massachusetts as a small boy with his widowed mother (whose son by a later marriage was Thomas Larkin, builder of the Larkin House in Monterey). Pursuing a mercantile career as a young man, Cooper arrived in Monterey in 1823 as master of his own sailing vessel. Three years later, he decided to make the coastal town his headquarters.

The sandy-haired New Englander, then in his early thirties, was short and unprepossessing. His left arm was withered by an injury in his early youth, causing him to be called *Juan el Manco* (the maimed) by the *Californios.* Still, he was as successful in his courtship of the charming Encarnacion, sister of Vallejo, as he was in his business; and in 1827, after his baptism in the Catholic Church as "Juan Bautista," he took the eighteen-year-old daughter of the Vallejos as his bride.

A shrewd businessman, Cooper soon acquired prestige as a merchant, as well as large acreage on the coast north of the Salinas River. In 1832, he built a second adobe on his Mon-

Glassed-in end gives wind protection.

Wallpaper was introduced in Monterey in the 1830s, about the same time this part of the Cooper house was built. The square piano is typical of those brought around the horn in the 1840s.

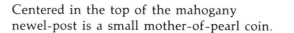

Centered in the top of the mahogany newel-post is a small mother-of-pearl coin.

terey property. This house, a long, one-story building on what is now Munras Avenue, was to be a home for his wife and children. Doña Encarnacion was well-satisfied with its setting, and before long, both her sister, Prudenciana, and her nephew, Juan Bautista Alvarado, were living only a few yards away, as first the Casa Amesti and then the larger of the two Alvarado townhouses were completed.

The locale would have been virtually a family corner, except that Cooper sold the northern half-section of his long adobe house to a stranger—the U.S. Consul to the Sandwich Islands, John C. Jones. Also included in the transaction was a strip of land, 40 by 183 feet, on present-day Polk Street, where the old storehouse stood. Ownership of these properties changed several times and did not return to the Cooper family for almost seventy years. During the first part of this interval, Doña Encarnacion had a variety of neighbors, as different tenants occupied the five-room apartment adjoining her home. But after 1845, it became the longtime home of the delightful Doña Luisa Estrada de Diaz, whose husband established a business in the Polk Street buildings.

Meanwhile, as Captain Cooper's affluence increased, he enlarged his portion of the building until, in the 1850s, it had become an impressive, two-story residence, with balcony overhanging the street. At the same time, the structures in the rest of the walled-in area took shape. Large barns were built for the family carriages, which entered through the massive gate on Munras Avenue. A small schoolhouse may also have stood on the grounds for the use of the Cooper girls, who were taught at home while the boys were sent to schools on the East coast and in Oahu.

Captain Cooper, who had added the Rancho El Sur as well as property in Sonoma to his holdings, continued his seafaring

Tile-covered shed sheltered *carretas.*

Barns were built for the family carriages. Other wooden structures for house servants were added in late 1800s.

Side gate opened onto Monterey's big gulch. Fruit trees inside wall have split with age but still blossom.

career, making many profitable voyages to the South Seas and the Orient. When in port, the genial, thickset little gentleman was well known both for his liberal hospitality and his eccentricities. On all occasions he was garbed in a blue sailor's jacket and gray satinet pants, with a white slouched hat and cowhide shoes completing the outfit. And a characteristic habit he had, when excited or vexed, was to bite at his maimed left hand.

In 1864, the Cooper family moved to San Francisco, where eight years later the Captain died. His widow and children inherited the Monterey property, and, eventually, the entire group of adobes came into the possession of his granddaughter, Frances Molera. At her death, in 1968, she willed the walled-in complex of buildings to the National Trust for Historic Preservation. The terms of the bequest provided that the Cooper home and adjoining one-story adobe be restored and maintained, but allowed for continued commercial use of the Polk Street property. Thus, this unique segment of old Monterey will remain a vibrant part of today's city.

Harbor shoreline originally came to the edge of the north porches.

The Custom House

Shortly after Mexico's declaration of independence from Spain, in 1821, the California ports of Monterey and San Diego were opened to foreign trade for the first time. The following spring saw the arrival of William Hartnell aboard the *John Begg* and the advent of a new era for Monterey. Henceforth, trading vessels from all over the world would bring bulging cargoes of "civilized" commodities to Monterey to exchange for hides and tallow. Import duties on foreign merchandise were substantial and became a major source of revenue for the government. And since custom officials were responsible for their collection, a Custom House was built as a control center where cargoes were registered.

Prior to 1827, several crude structures had been erected above the landing cove for the storage of supplies, but each in turn had fallen into ruins. The new building was constructed on the same site. It consisted of two rooms, the larger for a storeroom and the convenience of the corporal of the custom house guard, and the other for the guard corps. Built of adobe, with a peaked roof of sheet metal and tile, it was the first section of the present-day Custom House—the lower floor of the northern end. Adjacent to it were a hut fashioned of poles and tules for the use of the sailors and a shed to shield the small landing boats from the elements.

No significant changes were made in the Custom House until 1841, when Thomas Larkin contracted with the Mexican government to rebuild and enlarge the structure. Initial im-

Fireplace was added during restoration at the turn of the century.

provements included an addition of a second story on the north end, a portion of the center section, and a portico on the south side facing the bay. Larkin's charge for the construction was 2,300 pesos, half to be paid in coin and the balance in merchandise "from the first three ships required to pay duty at the port." Work continued until 1846, when most of the central part and the two-story southern wing were completed.

During the 1840s, the Custom House was the scene of many historic occasions, most notably, perhaps, the raising of the Stars and Stripes for the first time by Commodore Jones and, later, Commodore Sloat. In addition, the one-story middle section of the building became a center for gala social events. When a Yankee warship anchored in the harbor, a *baile grande* was held there, attended by all of Monterey's first families. Music was provided by the ship's military band and fine wines came from the hospitable Larkin. Commissioned officers mingled with the daughters of the elite, as they danced the fandango and *contradanza* until dawn. *Dueñas* relaxed their vigilance sufficiently to permit their charges to stroll unsupervised with the handsome young foreigners along the *corredor* fronting the bay.

After the mid-1860s, the building ceased to serve as a Custom House. For about thirty-five years, Captain Thomas Lambert and his wife served as custodians of the adobe while living in the southern section of the structure. Other portions of the building were rented for various purposes and, despite several attempts at repair, became completely dilapidated.

In 1900, a campaign for the restoration of the Custom House was begun by the Native Sons of the Golden West, who acquired temporary control of the property from the federal government. But in the 1930s, a group of concerned citizens had to raise funds for its purchase to prevent the government from selling it as surplus. Subsequently the historic building was renovated and deeded to the State. It has been refurbished and is now designated as State Historical Monument No. 1 and a National Customs Historic Landmark.

Open plaza gives new clear view of Custom House's land side.

Precise attention to early architectural detailing is evident in contemporary restoration.

The Estrada Adobe

José Mariano Estrada was a youth of twenty-two with the rank of ensign when he and his brother came to Monterey in 1806 as proteges of Governor Arrillaga. The favor of the governor, combined with Mariano's marriage to a daughter of the Arguello family, resulted in his rapid rise to a position of prominence. By the early 1820s, he had been granted two adjoining ranchos near the Salinas River and owned a large adobe on what is now Munras Avenue, near the adobe home of Captain Rogers Cooper. In the mid-1830s, concerned about providing for the two youngest of his ten children, Don José bought the house now called the Estrada adobe on present-day Tyler Street. The two-story, nine-room house was under construction at the time.

The Estrada adobe never served as a home for the youngsters for whom it had been purchased, but two of Estrada's older sons, José Ramon and Santiago, respectively held title to it. Then, in the 1870s, the house became the property of Santiago's daughter Juana and her husband, Francisco Watson, nicknamed Pancho. The Watsons converted the building into a hotel and called it the Pancho House.

The spacious house continued to serve as a hostelry for almost a hundred years, but with frequent changes of name and ownership. In 1879, as the St. Charles Hotel, it was described as a rambling, two-story adobe with "many rooms, bad cooking, and one bathroom." At the end of that year, a third story was added. In 1902, the building was leased for $35

a month by C. D. Casper, who subsequently purchased and remodeled it, adding a music hall and advertising "first class meals 25 cents and up." Casper's heirs further enlarged the hotel, naming it the Mission Inn, and as such it continued until 1961, when it was purchased by the Monterey Savings and Loan Association.

The firm restored the adobe to its original form, lavishing special attention to an exquisite rendering of architectural details. In addition, they erected a new building on the property which, with its bold, contemporary design, is a perfect complement to the massive simplicity of the old adobe. Dedicated to community use, the Estrada adobe is now not only an eloquent reminder of the past but a living part of the present.

Turned balusters and chamfered posts relate to many other Monterey adobes. Open patio, rare in the middle of any downtown, is result of restorative care.

Unique ridge construction allowed for small ports through which whales were sighted on the bay. Wooden north end could also serve as separate building.

The First Theatre

Although the long adobe building on Pacific Street is most noted as Monterey's first theatre and is still used as a playhouse, it was actually a precursor of the modern apartment dwelling. Close inspection of the facade and interior of the adobe section of the structure shows that it once was divided by hinged wooden partitions into self-contained apartment units. Four doors and four windows along the front of the adobe mark the divisions. Inside the building, a doorway opposite each exterior door led to a second room, with a fireplace for cooking as well as heat, and a rear exit. A large loft or attic was originally reached by two stairways in the building, one of which still stands at the north end of the theatre.

This highly functional arrangement provided for four two-room flats as well as for the possibility of two larger apartments with a loft room above each. In addition, because the wooden partitions could be raised and fastened to the ceiling, the adobe could be converted into an assembly room or a theatre. The utilitarian aspects of the structure were further enhanced by the separate nature of its northern frame segment which could be used as a store or bar.

The owner and builder of this unusual adobe was Jack Swan, a sailor who came to Monterey in 1843 after eleven adventurous years on the high seas. The genial little Scotsman, with his merry blue eyes and ready smile, soon became popular with the transient seamen of the port and decided to take advantage of his numerous friendships by opening a shop and

Following old photographs of a storage shed originally on Jack Swan's property, the State of California recently constructed, in adobe, a storehouse for use by the players of the First Theatre.

boardinghouse. He first built the small wooden structure, then added the adobe wing, which was completed in 1847.

Late in the 1840s, glamor came to Swan's versatile adobe when it first was used as the scene of theatrical performances. The partitions were raised and the long, high-ceilinged room resounded to the rousing thespian efforts given by members of Colonel Jonathan Stevenson's Seventh Regiment of New York Volunteers. Notable among their achievements was the production, in February 1850, of an adaptation of Shakespeare's *Henry IV* entitled The *Story of the Gadshill Robbery.* The scenery and curtain were painted by Lieutenant Alfred Sully, son of the famous artist Thomas Sully, and music was provided by the military band. The house was jammed, with a large crowd listening from outside the building.

The playhouse at that time was called the "Union Theatre", and from it Swan received a goodly rent. Another source of income came with the advent of the whaling industry in 1854, when Captain John Davenport housed his whalers in the loft of the adobe. But the principal use of the building over the years was as living quarters, generally for the less affluent families of Monterey. In the 1880s, Swan lost his property, and the kind-hearted old bachelor lived out his years plagued by poverty and deafness. A familiar figure in the town, with "pioneer of '43" plainly inscribed on his hatband, he subsisted on handouts from tourists whom he told about the old days.

Meanwhile, his building had fallen into disrepair. In 1906 it was purchased with funds provided by William Randolph Hearst and subsequently deeded to the state as a museum. With the opening performance of the "Troupers of the Gold Coast" in 1937, the old adobe once again became a theatre, featuring regular performances of colorful nineteenth-century melodrama.

Storehouse adobe is well chunked with bits of field stone, which helps it look older than it is.

The House of the Four Winds

Located towards the southern end of the 390-foot strip of land acquired by Thomas Oliver Larkin in the mid-1830s, this small adobe, named for the handwrought iron weather vane on its sloping roof, may have been the first building erected on his property. Very likely used as a store while his home was still under construction, it was subsequently rented out, and, in January, 1850, was sold along with the rest of the property that included the Larkin house, to Jacob Primer Leese.

The adobe enjoys the distinction of having been the first Hall of Records in the newly created County of Monterey. William Johnson, who served as County Recorder in 1850, had his office in the building, and later he made his home there when newly wed to Louisa Cano, stepdaughter of James Stokes. The Johnsons' son, Robert, later purchased the Larkin House from Rosanna Leese.

In October of 1868, Leese sold the House of Four Winds to his son, Jacob R. Leese, for $300. The following year it was purchased at four times that amount by the Martins of Carmel Valley. Almost half a century of vicissitudes ensued for the little house, until, in 1914, it was acquired by the Women's Civic Club of Monterey. Restored and authentically furnished, it now serves as a meeting place for a number of organizations.

Hipped roof has been severely compromised by slope of the roof over north section, now entryway.

The French Consulate

For forty-nine-year-old Jacques Antoine Moerenhout, his appointment as Consul of France at Monterey in 1846 was the culmination of a long and adventurous career. Born in the Netherlands, he had served as a youth in Napoleon's army, made and lost several fortunes in Chile, and spent more than a decade in Tahiti promoting expansion of the French empire. During part of this sojourn, and before his marriage to a young Chilean girl, he had been involved in an intimate friendship with a Tahitian island queen, Pomare. An expert miniature portraitist and a civil engineer, he was also a noted scholar. His research and writings on the South Sea Islands had earned him the reputation of an authority in the field, and as a result, President Andrew Jackson had appointed him as his Tahitian consul, a post Moerenhout held from 1835 to 1839.

When he arrived in Monterey from Tahiti to take up his post as French consul, he still bore the scars of an attempt upon his life by a political assassin who had mortally wounded his wife. For a time, he resided in the home of ex-Governor Alvarado. Then, in 1848, he purchased a lot on what is now Fremont Street and built a commodious adobe. It was a spacious home with a beautiful rose garden and fine plantings of shrubs and trees. Financial difficulties forced him to mortgage the property, and while he was away on an official visit to France in 1851, his home was sold in a public auction. He continued to serve as the French consular agent from other quarters in Monterey until 1859, when his office was transferred to Los Angeles.

The new owner of the long, low adobe was Captain Charles Wolter, a dashing ex-seaman who had spent his early years sailing around the world. On one of his visits to the port of Monterey, he had met and married Joséfa Estrada de Gomez, a young widow with five children. At first they made their home on the Rancho El Toro, 5,600 acres of property which belonged to Joséfa's family, and later lived in a large, two-story house on Alvarado Street. The former French Consulate, probably purchased for investment, was used as rental property. Then, in 1855, Wolter sold the property to Henry Blankman, whose wife was a Vallejo.

After the turn of the century, when the property had changed hands again, the house was neglected and fell into disrepair. In 1934, when it was about to be torn down, the city of Monterey and the Monterey History and Art Association joined forces to preserve the historic adobe. Through their efforts, the building was carefully reconstructed at its present location in El Estero Park.

Building has been moved in sections from original location.

The Gutiérrez Adobes

About twenty years elapsed between the construction of the two adjoining adobes that stand at the south end of Calle Principal. The two-story adobe nearest the corner was built by Joaquín Gutiérrez at the beginning of the 1840s. The contiguous wood and adobe structure was erected in the mid-1860s by one of his sons-in-law, John Miller.

Gutiérrez came to Monterey from Mexico while still in his teens. Nephew of General Nicolas Gutiérrez, who twice in the 1830s was acting governor of California, the young Joaquín enjoyed a moderately successful military career. In 1839, he married the sixteen-year-old María Joséfa Escobar, sister of a famous trio of hunters who captured grizzlies alive for the bull and bear fights in Monterey. Two years later, Gutiérrez, then twenty-five, received the grant of a town lot on which he built his adobe.

It was a comfortable dwelling, consisting of a large parlor, a dining room, and a bedroom on the lower floor, and an inside staircase leading from the dining room to the upper rooms. Behind the house was a walled-in garden and orchard containing a shed for the kitchen, which had an earthen floor. A balcony graced the front of the building.

Next door to the Gutiérrezes was a small adobe building known as the "priest's house." Its original owner, Graciano Manjares, had traded the house for the fruit orchard and "eight rooms and a parlor" in the buildings of the Mission San Carlos, which after secularization was a prey to such transactions. Thus, the adobe became the residence of the parish priest. After several subsequent changes in ownership, the property was purchased, in 1866, by John Miller, a butcher and grocer who had married Ramona Gutiérrez, one of the fifteen Gutiérrez offspring. He constructed a new house on the site, making the north wall common to both dwellings.

The two adobes remained in the family and were the subject of much litigation among the many Gutiérrez heirs after the death of Joséfa, who outlived Joaquín by more than twenty years. In 1945, the original adobe built by Joaquín Gutiérrez was purchased by the Monterey Foundation and given to the State of California. Designated as an historical monument, it has been restored and is rented for commercial purposes. The later portion of the building, the adobe built by John Miller, is privately owned and is also used as business property.

Careful restoration and contemporary additions
have transformed sheepherder's dwelling into a
gracious home.

The Jacks Adobe

On an eight-acre, oak-wooded tract of the Rancho Aguajito is a gracious adobe sometimes called the Casa de Castro. The date of its construction is not known, but the rancho was purchased by José Antonio María Castro in 1853. That same year, Castro left for Mexico, never to return. Before departing he sold his newly acquired property to Antonia Emma Moerenhout, but within two days of the sale his wife bought two-thirds of it back. Eight years later, the entire rancho was in the possession of David Jacks. Up to this point there is no evidence of an adobe on the land.

During the 1860s, the rancho was used for sheep raising, and it is possible that the present-day adobe was built for sheepherders. After the death of David Jacks, in 1909, much of the rancho was subdivided, but his daughter, Margaret Jacks, kept the old adobe and surrounding acreage. Over a period of time, starting in the 1930s, she painstakingly restored the building. To insure authenticity, ancient techniques were employed, such as mixing the pulp of cactus plants with the whitewash used on the walls. The same care was exercised in the creation of the gardens, to which cuttings from beautiful old Monterey rose bushes were transplanted. Structures added to the property, like the bedroom wing built on to the adobe and the separate guest house, were designed to match the original architecture.

Large square tiles are similar to those found in original mission construction.

The old house was Miss Jacks' home whenever she was in the Monterey area, and on it she lavished her love of the land where she had spent most of her life. She died in 1962, having donated much property for public use, but her *casa querida* was left to a cousin. Today, still privately owned and cherished, it evokes the essence of a more tranquil time.

The Lara Adobe

Built before 1849, the one-story adobe that stands on present-day Pierce Street, between Franklin and Jefferson, in Monterey, has had a long and varied history. Owned for over fifty years by a woman, Feliciana Lara, who obtained title to the property by act of the *ayuntamiento* of Monterey in September, 1849, it was sold for delinquent taxes after her death in 1905. In the interim, its story is obscure. Some say that the building was sold to a Jesús Soto in the 1850s, but the property described as being assessed to him was recorded as "one adobe back of Colton Hall", which is not the location of Doña Feliciana's dwelling.

North of the Lara adobe were the homes of Doña Antonia Vallejo, a next-door neighbor, and of Feliciano Soberanes, at the corner of Franklin and Pierce. Records show that in the 1890s, the Lara house was occupied by an elderly Indian couple named Manuel and Felicidad Soto. They were in straitened circumstances, and old Manuel always welcomed the chance to earn a "two bit piece" by bringing a couple of bags of pitch from the woods above Monterey. Best of his customers were the de la Torres, who lived down the street.

In 1919, the property was purchased by Josephine Blanch, an artist and curator of the Hotel Del Monte Art Gallery, who remodeled the building but preserved the simplicity of its original lines. A touch of glamor came to the old house in 1944, when it was acquired by John Steinbeck. The author lived in it briefly with his second wife and their infant son. Now used for medical offices, the building is in excellent condition. Shadowed by the spreading branches of an enormous old cypress tree, it stands as a fine example of the charm that abides in clean-cut, early adobe architecture.

Giant cypress has grown to almost overwhelm small street-side adobe.

Despite many changes in detail, Larkin House still provides a dominant focus for contemporary architecture in California.

The Larkin House

The adobe that pioneered the distinctive style of architecture known as Monterey Colonial was built by a Yankee merchant, Thomas Oliver Larkin. Larkin came to California in 1832, at the suggestion of his half-brother, John Rogers Cooper. Landing at Yerba Buena, he found the small settlement too tame for his taste and moved on to the bustling trade center of Monterey. In the autumn of 1833, the thirty-one-year-old Larkin married Rachel Holmes, an attractive young widow whom he had met enroute from Boston, and the newlyweds lived, first, on the Cooper ranch and then in half of the William Hartnell home in Monterey. Finally, in January of 1835, Larkin requested a town lot, not far from the residence of his half-brother, and began assembling materials for a home of his own.

The Larkin house was under construction for three years and cost approximately $5,000. Included in the expenditure was room and board for the workmen, which was customary at the time, and such sundry incidentals as "Rum for Raising the roof". Newly arrived Scotch and Irish immigrants provided the skilled labor, while Indians did the menial tasks. The design of the house exhibited a masterful adaptation of the architectural design of the Eastern Seaboard to the building materials native to California. The mainstay of the materials used was adobe brick, but a strong redwood frame made possible an upper story and greater freedom in the placement of windows. The floor plan followed the American colonial tra-

Millsaw marks on post and board indicate restoration materials. Small square is recent carpenter's decoration.

Dining room was originally used as Larkin store.

Much of the glass in the house is original. Small panes were used to reduce breakage.

dition of two rooms opening off either side of a central passageway, from which a staircase led to the upper story. The hipped roof, covered with shingles, was also in accord with New England tradition. But the redwood veranda and balcony, constructed to protect the two-story adobe walls from water erosion, were reminiscent of the Southern plantation. The finished house boasted two fireplaces—one of which was upstairs—as well as wallpaper, milled doors, and small-paneled glass windows of double-sash design.

The Larkin family occupied the house while it was still in an unfinished state and then made it their home for fourteen years. For Larkin it was the center of his trading operations as well as his residence. He quickly expanded his business interests and became one of the wealthiest and most influential men in the region. Before long he also took on the role of foremost advocate of peaceable American annexation of California; and in 1844, when he was appointed United States Consul, his home became the headquarters of the official and social life of the capital. During the Constitutional Convention, the Larkin dinner table was always set to entertain at least ten delegates a day. The gracious Mrs. Larkin also gave gala parties upstairs, in what is now displayed as a bedroom. One guest recalls Mrs. Larkin bringing in large pumpkins to serve as extra seats among the elegant furnishings imported from New England.

Late in 1849, Larkin decided to move to the booming new city of San Francisco and sold the house and adjoining property for $30,000. The new owner was Jacob Primer Leese, a business partner from Sonoma. At that time, Leese was exceedingly affluent, but eventually he lost most of his money and property, including his wife Rosalia's sizeable dowry. Bitter domestic quarrels ensued and Leese left for Texas to recoup his fortunes. Meanwhile, to help support the family, Leese's eldest daughter, Rosanna, built a two-story frame boarding-house, adjoining the Larkin House. It was there that Robert Louis Stevenson stayed when he first came to Monterey in 1879. The structure was removed some years later.

Shortly after the turn of the century, the Larkin House was sold to Robert Johnson, an attorney who, for many years, was mayor of Monterey. Bon vivant and generous host, Johnson, with his wife, the former Teresa Trescony, made the house a mecca for artists and visiting dignitaries from all over the world. Then in 1922, when the property was once again offered for sale, it was purchased by a grandaughter of Thomas Larkin. Mrs. Alice Larkin Toulmin carefully renovated and preserved the venerable adobe, furnishing it with many fine old pieces among which were some that had belonged to her grandfather. In 1957, she deeded the house to the State as an historical monument, and so it stands to commemorate the beginning of Monterey Colonial architecture.

In the midst of still-cultivated orchard land, the spacious Martinez adobe glows in elegant refinement.

The Martinez Adobe

On the John Muir National Historic Site, sharing honors with the residence of the renowned naturalist, is a spacious adobe built over a hundred years ago. The land on which it stands was once part of the 17,786-acre Rancho El Pinole, granted in 1824 to Ignacio Martinez, then a ranking officer at the presidio of San Francisco, who had seen thirty-four years of military service. In 1831, he retired and soon after settled on the grant with his wife and eight children, living in a simple adobe long since reclaimed by the soil.

When death came to the old soldier, in 1848, and the rancho was divided among his sons and daughters, Vicente, the second-oldest son, inherited the portion near the newly established town of Martinez. There in the beautiful Alhambra Valley, amidst gently sloping, green-mantled hills, Don Vicente built a two-story adobe home for his second wife, to whom he had been married only a year.

About the same time, another pair of newlyweds came to live in the valley. Vicente's sister, María Encarnacion, became the bride of a young rancher, Abeline Altamirano, and in 1850 they built a small adobe on her portion of the rancho. But within a few years, both the Altamiranos and Vicente Martinez lost their adobe homesteads. Financial difficulties following American annexation forced Don Vicente to sell his home, and Doña Encarnacion's adobe went for $780 at auction.

Meanwhile, in 1853, John Strentzel, a Polish physician destined to become a famed horticulturist, arrived in the Alhambra Valley and purchased over 800 acres of the Rancho El Pinole. With his wife and daughter, he settled in a simple frame farmhouse on the southern part of the property. About twenty years later he bought the Vicente Martinez adobe, using it as quarters for ranch employees. Shortly after his daughter's marriage to John Muir, in 1880, Dr. Strentzel built the large Victorian mansion which stands within sight of the Martinez adobe. After 1890, the Strentzel house became the Muir residence, and in later years, one of Muir's daughters lived in the Martinez adobe with her husband and three sons.

In 1881, a close friend of John Muir, the well-known educator John Swett, purchased the little adobe that once had belonged to Doña Encarnacion, along with 180 acres of surrounding land. The house has been greatly altered and enlarged, but the original adobe is still part of the present-day structure. The large, two-story Vicente Martinez adobe has been beautifully preserved. In 1955, it was purchased by the Contra Costa Historical Society as a headquarters and museum. Though these plans were not fully realized, the elegant house, adorned with graceful balconies and set amidst acres of orchard and vineyard, is a charming asset to the John Muir National Historic Site. The National Park Service, to whom it now belongs, plans to refurbish the interior of the adobe and open it to the public.

The house of gold, built by Thomas Larkin.

Casa del Oro

Best known as the Boston Store, the tile-roofed adobe in back of the Pacific House was built in the 1840s on a lot granted to Thomas Larkin. Subsequently, the property was purchased by José Ábrego, in 1848, and leased for use as a general merchandise store to Joseph Boston. Boston was a civilian employee who arrived with the military contingent accompanying Brigadier General Bennett Riley in the spring of 1849.

An experienced merchant, Boston had a good credit rating with business firms in the far corners of the globe and was able to establish a large and varied stock of goods. Soon the small building was bulging with every item that the citizens of Monterey might conceivably require—not only cutlery and crockery but everything from a tooth brush to a rat trap. Nothing was too large or too small to be stocked—from pearl buttons to blacksmith bellows—it was all available. Small wonder that the store prospered.

Boston was also shrewd in his choice of competent employees. Less than a year after opening the store, he hired as a clerk the man destined to become Monterey's wealthiest landowner—David Jacks. Newly arrived in the community, Jacks was grateful for the job and devoted to his employer. A warm friendship developed between the two men, and though Jacks soon went into business for himself, he always harbored a sentimental attachment for the establishment where he had received kindness and respect.

In an exceptionally small building, lack of complications and adornment in design speak of a singular dignity.

Greatly altered facade still retains an aura of welcome.

Modern fountain and open plaza now make it possible to see the full sweep of The Pacific House.

The Pacific House

Monterey in the 1840s was a thriving seaport, its harbor a regular port of call for whaling ships and commercial vessels plying the Pacific waters. The enterprising Thomas Larkin, who cultivated the friendship of shipmasters from the far-flung corners of the globe, saw the advantage of acquiring waterfront property in the town and, in 1843, purchased a large piece of land near the harbor from Doña Carmen Ruiz de Ferguson. An adobe house which stood on the property is believed to have been the original segment, or northern section, of the present-day Pacific House.

The following year, Larkin invested several thousand dollars in the property, walling in the area and constructing two wells in anticipation of supplying water to ships at anchor in the bay. Then, when Monterey was occupied by American forces and Larkin was appointed Naval Agent and Storekeeper for the United States government, his facility on the beach became an official supply depot and he hastened to enlarge it further. In June 1847, a contract was let for construction of the southern section of the Pacific House. Improvements were also made in the wells, one of which was enclosed in the south end of the new building—just inside the lower front door. Its indoor location provided protection from contamination and made its water supply especially desirable. The second well was situated in the walled-in area back of the building about a foot to the side of the present-day false well.

All lower floor rooms open onto the *corredor*.

Garden, which used to be the bull and bear area, now forms a gracious setting for many festivities.

When the focal point for commercial development along the Pacific Coast shifted to San Francisco in 1849, Larkin sold the Pacific House to James McKinley, a Scotch sailor who had separated from his ship in Santa Barbara and subsequently migrated to Monterey. There, he married Carmen Amesti, daughter of Doña Prudenciana, and became a successful businessman. At his store in the two-story Alvarado adobe, which he had also purchased, McKinley gave employment to a fellow Scotsman recently arrived in Monterey, David Jacks, who was later to acquire the Pacific House for himself.

In 1850, the Pacific House became a hostelry for seafaring men and sported a flourishing tavern on its street floor. At the same time, offices of the newly organized County of Monterey were housed in the building. About the middle of the decade, hard times hit Monterey, with a concomitant spurt of foreclosures and sheriff's sales. McKinley's holdings were sold to satisfy a judgment for unpaid debts in excess of $34,000, and a portion of the Pacific House came into the possession of Jane Allen Krampner. She operated the tavern during the 1860s, when bull and bear fights were held in the corral back of the building and staid newspaper and attorneys' offices occupied the second floor.

In 1880, the entire piece of property was acquired by the Scottish merchant, David Jacks, by this time one of Monterey's wealthiest citizens. He used the Pacific House principally for storage, stacking lumber to the ceilings and crowding heavy equipment into the first-floor rooms. After his death in 1909, his daughters restored the building and transformed the weed-choked backyard into a beautiful garden. Margaret Jacks, one of the daughters, deeded the property to the State of California in 1954, and today it is a fine museum, with festive gatherings held in the former bull and bear arena, now called Memory Garden.

Modern restoration reflects Spanish influence.

Typical Spanish patio flooring is composed of recently made bricks and tiles.

The Sánchez Adobe

In present-day Pacifica, a mile east of the coast highway, stands a commodious two-story adobe built in 1846, of sun-dried bricks—some of which were made by mission Indians as early as 1786. Built as the home of Francisco Sánchez, it occupies the site of an old mission quadrangle which was the first outpost of civilization in what is now San Mateo County.

In the mid-1780s, a crop and cattle rancho for San Francisco's Mission Dolores was established in the fertile valley of San Pedro. A chapel was erected and foundations laid for a large complex of buildings. About 400 Indian neophytes were moved to the new location, wheat and vegetables were planted, and soon thousands of cattle roamed the adjacent hills. But a few years later, an epidemic decimated the Indian population and the agricultural operation had to be abandoned. Then, in 1834, with secularization, the mission lost its lands, which were now open to petitioners of the government.

By 1835, José Antonio Sánchez, a retired soldier of the San Francisco presidio, had occupied the 14,639-acre Rancho Buri Buri, which adjoined the mission property. That same year his son Francisco asked for title to the 8,926 acres that lay over the ridge to the west of Buri Buri, and finally, in 1839, was granted the Rancho San Pedro, which covered some seven miles of coastline.

On the spot where the crumbling remains of the mission chapel still stood, Don Francisco built a fine, six-room residence, utilizing bricks from the adobe ruins. There, in 1846, he established his home with his wife, Teodora, and their four children.

Sánchez, then in his early forties, a ranking officer in the military and several times *alcalde* of the budding town of San Francisco, was also one of the five wealthiest men in the area. Naturally, the Sánchez adobe became the scene of many a brilliant social gathering, attended by such prominent persons as former Governor Alvarado and John C. Frémont. But the American occupation brought severe financial reverses. Though Sánchez managed to keep the Rancho San Pedro intact throughout his lifetime, soon after his death, in 1862, strangers took possession of his home.

The Sánchez family leased the rancho to an American, Francis Sievers, who lived in the adobe and sub-leased portions of the land for truck farming. Later the property changed hands and the land was subdivided. Then, in 1879, General Edward Kirkpatrick, a veteran of the Civil War, acquired the house and some surrounding acreage. Once again the old adobe came alive with loving care. Renovated and landscaped, it was the general's residence for a number of years. But when he moved to Europe, tenants neglected the fine old building and it fell into disrepair. Its many uses after the turn of the century included that of bootleg bar and what might politely be called "hotel". At the end, it was reduced to a packing shed and bunk house for farm workers.

Finally, in 1946, Kirkpatrick's widow sold the property. A year later, through the efforts of the San Mateo Historical Society, it was purchased by the County of San Mateo. Today, beautifully restored and furnished as a museum, it looks much as it did when it was the home of the Sánchez family and a center for the social life of the early rancheros.

The Adobes of San Juan Bautista

Padres viewed the activities of the plaza from their living quarters fronting on the arcade and adjacent to the church.

Like a subtle fragrance, the ambiance of *los dias de antes* hovers over the spacious, sunlit plaza of San Juan. Three sides of the quadrangle are formed by ancient adobes, all but one of which originated under the sovereignty of Spain. At the open end of the square is the wide vista of San Benito Valley, little changed through the centuries. Below the mesa on which the plaza stands circles a segment of the King's Highway, the original Camino Real, that once linked the missions of Spanish California. In this serene setting there is a stillness and a waiting, and out of it emerges the story of how this place came into being.

It began with the founding of Alta California's fifteenth mission, on June 24th, the feast day of Saint John the Baptist in 1797. The first structures were a temporary church and living quarters for the padres. From these crude beginnings came the great rectangular church and the long arcaded monastery which together form the bold facade to the west of the plaza. Built by Indian labor under supervision of the friars, they were completed in 1812. Next to be built were barracks to house the soldiers and a dormitory to insure safekeeping of unmarried Indian women of the mission. The soldiers' quarters consisted of a one-story adobe with an adjoining two-story guard house, the site of the future Plaza Hotel. The "nunnery" for Indian maids stood across from the monastery on land later occupied by Plaza Hall. Both buildings were constructed by 1815, completing the outlines of the plaza.

Placement of cross and bell always preceded
construction of the church.

Ancient walls show ravages of many earth tremors.

divided the mission properties, then took the further step of auctioning them off to friends and relatives. His son, José Antonio María, who skyrocketed to political prominence as the close friend and ally of Governor Alvarado, also acted to take advantage of the situation. In 1839, when he was appointed prefect of the First District, which comprised all of northern California, he designated San Juan Bautista as his headquarters and called the incipient town San Juan de Castro. A year later, he ordered construction of a two-story adobe, next door to the barracks, which would serve as his residence and the administrative office of the district.

Beautiful in its simplicity, the Castro house was a fine example of California adobe architecture. Two rooms flanked a central hallway—the large *sala* opened into the office. Upstairs were three bedrooms. Back of the house stood several small structures that housed the kitchen, servants' quarters, and storehouses. Graceful balconies that seemed "almost to float on air" spanned the width of the building.

Here the popular Don José Castro, with his lovely wife, Modesta, and their charming children, held court during the first half of the 1840s. His home became a gathering place for neighboring rancheros, and on Sundays the hard-packed dirt plaza was filled to overflowing with ox teams, *carretas,* and saddle horses. People from all over the countryside flocked to Mass, and many spent the rest of the day at the Casa de Castro. During fiestas the plaza was enclosed by a stout wooden stockade for the bear and bull fights. Two adjoining stakes were driven into the ground, to one of which a bear was chained by a hind foot, and to the other a bull fastened by a front foot. Then the sport began, while high-spirited señoritas and their cheering escorts watched from the balcony of the Castro adobe.

Keeping pace with the building program was the cultivation of extensive orchards and gardens. At the foot of the hill, below the northeast end of the plaza, 800 pear trees were planted. Herds of livestock were raised to feed the growing Indian population, which increased to over a thousand souls.

For three decades the mission prospered in pastoral tranquility. Then, in 1835, secularization brought swift and sudden change. Control of mission affairs was transferred from the padres to a civil administrator, José Tiburcio Castro. Acting in accord with the government decree of secularization, he

Home and headquarters for the *comandante-general,*
this expansive adobe overlooks plaza and countryside.

By 1845, José Castro had been elevated to the rank of *coman-dante general* of California, but his days of glory were numbered. American occupation was imminent. The following year, John Frémont encamped with a contingent of buckskin-clad warriors on the slopes of Gavilan Peak overlooking San Juan Bautista. At his headquarters, Castro assembled a force of 200 men and threatened to drive out the *bandoleros.* Before a showdown occurred, Frémont evacuated his position, moving on to the Sacramento Valley. But within a matter of months California had been occupied by the victorious armies of the United States, and the stars and stripes flew over the plaza of Castro's San Juan. Yet, the once proud general seemed to harbor slight resentment towards the people of the country that had humiliated him. In February of 1848, days after the Mexican-American war had officially ended, he offered his home rent-free to a destitute family from Iowa.

Survivors of the ill-fated Donner party, the Breen family arrived in San Juan penniless and scarcely recovered from the shock of their ordeal. Patrick Breen, in his late fifties and in poor health, was faced with finding a way to house and sup-

Early morning mist softens the fine detail of
San Juan's early hotel.

port his wife and seven children—the youngest of whom was a baby. He had left a prosperous career in the Midwest for the beckoning promise of California. The household had started their journey with three wagons loaded with provisions and furnishings, as well as a small herd of livestock. All had been lost along the way. After months of starvation and exposure in the snows of a Sierra winter, the battered little group had wandered through the central valleys, seeking a place to settle. The great generosity of José Castro must have seemed like a miracle to the Breens, who were devout Catholics. They had additional cause to give thanks later that same year.

When word reached San Juan that gold had been discovered in the Sierra foothills, the sixteen-year-old John Breen set out to try his luck. By December he was back with more than $10,000 worth of gold dust! The Breens purchased the Castro adobe and for a time operated it as the United States Hotel, a very popular inn for travelers on their way to the goldfields. The hostelry charged five dollars a night "for entertaining a man and his beast." Before long the Breens were able to buy some 400 acres of prime agricultural land in the area. Once again they were well-off, and succeeding generations of the family occupied the house as a residence.

The gold rush brought a swift and burgeoning prosperity to the sleepy town of San Juan. Three thoroughfares from San Francisco to Los Angeles intersected at the site of the old mission, and seven stage lines made the plaza their stopping place. Ranchers brought cattle and sheep by the thousands to San Juan, where they were sold to wholesale butchers from San Francisco and San Jose. Hotels sprang up to accommodate the influx of travelers.

In 1855, an enterprising Italian decided to capitalize on the bonanza. Angelo Zanetta was a superb chef, skilled in both Italian and French cuisine. He had worked at the St. Charles Hotel in New Orleans as well as the Washington Hotel in Monterey. Now he took over and refurbished the Sebastopol Hotel, back of what had been the barracks. This was merely a step towards larger endeavors: the following year on the celebration of San Juan's birthday, he set up a bar in the large corner room of the old barracks, and in twenty-four hours took in three thousand dollars. Naturally, he lost little time in opening negotiations to acquire the property for a hotel, and obtained a lease for use of the building.

Combining the barracks and the adjoining guard house, he added a wooden second story to the corner adobe and thus constructed a spacious hotel. The Plaza Hotel opened in 1858 with a gala celebration. From far and near, rancheros came with their families to see the new hostelry and partake of thick, juicy steaks smothered in mushrooms, a specialty of the house. A band played on the hotel veranda and the plaza was crowded with gaily attired *cabelleros* and sparkling señoritas. News of the fine foods and potables provided by the genial Zanetta soon spread and before long his hotel became the commercial and social center of the community.

As a one-story adobe, this was originally a dormitory for Indian maidens. In 1868, Angelo Zanetta and John Comfort reconstructed the building and opened it as a public hall.

In 1868, Zanetta thought it time to expand. The thriving town needed a public hall. His partner, John Comfort, had purchased the old adobe "nunnery" which had fallen into disrepair. Using the best of the adobe bricks, the partners reconstructed the building, adding a wooden upper story. Laid over 30-foot-long joists, the upstairs floor of Plaza Hall became famous for its springiness. Many a gala ball was held there, in addition to numerous political and civic gatherings. Eventually the first floor of the building was remodeled to become, for many years, a private residence for the Zanetta family. The elegantly furnished, nine-room apartment has been kept intact as part of the present-day Historic Park.

The old Zanetta house forms the eastern arm of the open quadrangle of historic adobes that comprise the San Juan Bautista Historical Monument. Created in 1933 by the California State Park Commission, the Monument also includes the Castro house, the Plaza Hotel, and the frame livery stable—once operated in connection with the Plaza Hotel and now equipped as a museum. Both the secular buildings, purchased and restored by the State, and the mission complex, restored under the expert supervision of Harry Downie, are superb examples of the California heritage. Today the plaza of San Juan stands as an island in time, where the past seems somehow more real than the present.

Casa Serrano

In the days when Monterey's Pacific Street was still called Calle Estrada, a "foreigner" named Thomas Larkin began construction of a three-room adobe house on the dusty lane. Before it was completed, Florencio Serrano, who was courting the spirited Rita de la Torre, bought it as a home for his future bride. Carefully he equipped the adobe with a few simple comforts, installing wooden floors and windows and building the customary outdoor, lean-to kitchen. It was a pleasing house, divided downstairs into a large center room, about 19 by 22 feet, and two smaller rooms at either end. A loft was reached by an outside, wooden stairway. In the summer of 1845, the happy couple began their residence in what was to be the home of the Serrano family for almost a century.

Eleven years earlier, Serrano had arrived in Monterey from Mexico City as a penniless youth of twenty, who had been a medical student before the death of his parents thrust him on his own resources. Eagerly he had grasped the opportunity to become a colonist and landowner, taking the arduous trip to California. There, bitter disappointment awaited him, as the glowing inducements given him and the other colonists turned into empty promises. To augment his problems, young Serrano was responsible for the support of an older sister, Francisca, and her two small children, all of whom had accompanied him.

The personable young man found employment as a clerk to the administrator of the San Antonio Mission, but he was overcome there by an affliction—a severe inflammation of the optic nerves—that confined him to a darkened room for several months and was to plague him all his life. He moved back to Monterey in search of medical attention, while his sister, Francisca, discouraged, returned with her children to Mexico. Serrano recovered and subsequently held various administrative posts in the capital, married Rita de la Torre, and built a promising career in the government service.

Meanwhile Francisca, who was inordinately attached to her brother, had returned to Mexico, exacting Serrano's pledge that he would follow her. Repeatedly she wrote upbraiding him for deceiving her. "You cannot imagine with what impatience and longing I await (your) arrival . . . I could die with rage . . . for if I had not believed you with such faith, I would never have left California without you." But Don Florencio, satisfied with his situation, was not inclined to listen to her pleas.

Then, shortly after the American occupation, his felicity came to an end. Though he had received important appointments under the new government such as successor to Walter Colton as *alcalde* of Monterey, he could not reconcile himself to the conquest of his country. The gentle, soft-spoken man

held himself aloof from the Americans and refused to compete in his new setting. In despair, he wrote Francisca that he would like to move back to Mexico with his family, but she urged him to try to get along where he was, as conditions in his homeland had become deplorable.

After a few unsuccessful business ventures, Serrano settled down to teaching, an occupation in which he had a sincere interest. But the school, conducted in his *casa,* yielded scant income for his family of six children. As his eyesight worsened, only his phenomenal memory made it possible for him to continue his work. At last, totally blind, he was supported by his sons until his death, in 1877, at the age of sixty-three.

Serrano's heirs lived on in the old adobe until 1933, when the property was leased to the Cademartoris for a unique restaurant. By 1959, the Casa Serrano was abandoned and in disrepair, when it was purchased by the Monterey History and Art Association. Today, restored and enlarged, it is the permanent home of the organization.

To reach children's sleeping loft Casa Serrano
has typical outside staircase.

Sherman's Quarters

Lowering of the street emphasizes view of chalk-rock used in adobe construction.

South of the Larkin house and separated from it by a small garden is a one-room adobe built at an unknown date by Thomas Larkin. One of several structures which stood on his property, it was for a brief period, in 1847, the headquarters of two successive military governors of California—General Stephen Kearny and Colonel Richard Mason. Kearny also resided in the Larkin house, as the guest of the United States Consul. When Colonel Mason assumed command, he was assisted in his administrative duties by two young officers destined to achieve renown—Lieutenants Henry Halleck and William Tecumseh Sherman. They shared quarters in the little adobe, until soon after the military headquarters was moved to *El Cuartel,* the former offices of the Mexican government, on present-day Munras Avenue.

The small structure saw many uses throughout the years. Most bizarre was that of storage space for an empty coffin! When Robert Johnson occupied the Larkin house, he allowed the awesome object to be stored there in a redwood box after its purchase at a bargain price by a Monterey woman who mistakenly thought her husband was about to die. It terrified most of the children in the neighborhood until finally it was removed, when Johnson converted the building into a billiard room. Today the adobe, equipped as a museum, is an integral part of the Larkin complex.

Deterioration of adobe plaster reveals two headers above door. Swooping tie-bolt decorates and contrasts with the rugged rock wall.

Casa Soberanes

In 1841, when José Rafael Papías Estrada built the two-story adobe now called the Casa Soberanes, he was a youth of twenty-one. A member of the illustrious Estrada family and grandson of the Vallejos, he was also a step-brother of Governor Alvarado. These influential family connections made it possible for him to obtain not only the large town lot on which he constructed the house but also a substantial land grant in the Salinas Valley a year later. Marriage in 1844 to Concepción Malarín, daughter of a wealthy merchant and landowner, added even more to his status in the community.

For over a decade, the Estradas lived in the six-room hillside adobe overlooking the bay, and it became a center for social gatherings of Monterey's most prominent families. A frequent visitor was Ezequiel Soberanes, a cousin of Don José Rafael. Both Soberanes and his wife, María Ignacia, were charmed by the Estrada house and, when the Estradas suffered temporary financial reverses, Soberanes bought the property.

Seven of the Soberanes children were born in the spacious adobe. Among them was the beautiful, dark-eyed Bersabe, who, while the family was staying at their second home on the south coast, met and married Tom Slate, owner of land at the hot springs which today is known as Esalen. The newlyweds built a home there, but life on the precipitous sea-wall below Big Sur proved too rugged for Bersabe, especially after she had begun to raise a brood of youngsters. The Slates therefore moved to Monterey, where they constructed a commodious frame dwelling next door to the Casa Soberanes. The Slate home stood where present-day Del Monte Avenue passes the old adobe.

Again, the Casa Soberanes came alive with the sound of children, as Bersabe's youngsters played around the well in the front yard or helped their grandmother in the rear vegetable garden. There, many hours were spent grinding the corn that grew tall against the back wall, or preparing bright red peppers to dry in the sun. Undoubtedly, all domestic routine was forgotten on the great day in 1899 when their neighbor to the north, Lou Henry, married the young Herbert Hoover. After the reception, Mrs. Henry came across the vacant lot between the houses, bringing leftover delicacies for the Slate children.

Bersabe's elder brother, Ezequiel Jr., inherited the house. He had no children and, after his death, his widow sold the property in 1922 to Jean Booth. She made the fine old adobe her home, restoring the building and creating beautiful terraced gardens. While she lived there, she married Reuben Serrano, grandson of the Don Florencio who had built the Casa Serrano.

In 1941, the Casa Soberanes became the property of William and Mayo Hayes O'Donnell. Both were devoted to the preservation of Monterey's architectural heritage, and Mr. O'Donnell, then managing editor of the *Monterey Peninsula Herald,* wrote many a stirring article on the subject while watching the inspiring view from the balcony of his home. Today the house is an outstanding example of that heritage, and so it will remain, because Mrs. O'Donnell has given it to the State of California to be maintained as an historical monument.

Original mission church fell to the ground. When Mariano Vallejo came to Sonoma, he took what had been a storeroom and made it into a chapel.

The Adobes of Sonoma

North of the Golden Gate, in the Valley of the Moon, lies a land of rolling hills rich with oak and laurel, threaded by curving, crystalline streams and deep in fragrant grasses. Here stood Mexico's northernmost outpost of Empire, stronghold against Russian encroachment in California. It was established at the Pueblo of Sonoma by the man whose name became synonymous with the Northern Frontier - Mariano Guadalupe Vallejo.

Descendant of proud Spanish *conquistadores,* Mariano was born in Monterey, in 1807, eighth child of Ignacio Vicente Ferrer Vallejo, the hard-bitten pioneer soldier, and Doña María Antonia, gently reared daughter of the Lugos. Personable and intelligent, the young Vallejo was favored with an unusually fine education, partly as the protege of Governor Solá. He began his military career as a cadet, at the age of sixteen, and by the time he was twenty-three, he had advanced to the position of *comandante* of the presidio of San Francisco. The following year, marriage to the beautiful Francisca Benicia Carrillo made him a member of another distinguished California family.

In 1833, impressed by the competence of the youthful officer, Governor Figueroa dispatched Vallejo to inspect Russian activity at Fort Ross. He returned to recommend colonization of northern California as the best means of arresting progress of the Russian settlements. As a result, Vallejo was commissioned to lay out a pueblo in the valley of Sonoma and given the task of administering the secularization of the Mission San Francisco Solano.

Last and most northerly of the mission chain, San Francisco Solano had been established in 1823 as an earlier attempt to stem the Russian advance. An impressive array of adobe buildings were erected, including a church, monastery, shops and storerooms. But harsh treatment of the Indian neophytes caused an uprising, and many of the structures were severely damaged by fire. The once-prosperous mission never fully recovered, and by the time Vallejo arrived as *comisionado,* it was virtually abandoned.

Using a pocket compass to survey the future town of Sonoma, Vallejo laid out a large plaza of about eight acres. On its northeast corner stood the old mission buildings. Acting as his own engineer, Vallejo outlined streets and divided the projected pueblo into lots. In the same month that Vallejo was laying the foundations of the pueblo, a grateful governor granted him ten leagues of land nearby. This was the Rancho Petaluma, which eventually would include over 100 square miles. Standing on a hilltop overlooking his vast domain, Vallejo rejoiced that this magnificent valley would become his homeland. On December 2, 1834, he established his military company at Sonoma, and in June of the following year he brought his pregnant wife, Francisca, and baby son to the lonely outpost.

The only housing available was in rooms of the abandoned mission. There his first daughter was born in August, 1835. It was time to build a proper home for his family. Construction of the *Casa Grande* began early in 1836 on a parcel of land west of the mission. Two stories high, with a three-story lookout tower, the adobe was remarkable for its time and place. A broad veranda extended across the building, and there were

Balcony of Indian servants' quarters, behind *Casa Grande.*

numerous spacious rooms. To the rear, a long, low adobe was the kitchen and servants' quarters. Still further back were orchards and a garden. Soon the palatial residence became a mecca for distinguished visitors who remarked upon its lavish furnishings and elegant life-style. Doña Francisca, who "each year had either a baby next to her heart or on her lap", was fully occupied in supervising a large retinue of Indian servants, five of whom were required just to grind corn for the tortillas.

Between the *Casa Grande* and the mission church, Vallejo erected a two-story adobe barracks for his troops. Gradually other adobes were built around the square. First of these was the home of Don Mariano's brother, Salvador, who had taken as his bride Maria de la Luz Carrillo, sister of Francisca. Completed in 1840, it was directly west of the *Casa Grande.* A short time later, Don Salvador built a second adobe opposite the northwest corner of the plaza. Eventually it would become the El Dorado Hotel. Then, in the mid-1840s, Jacob Primer Leese, husband of Mariano's sister, added a fine adobe house on the southwest side of the plaza. Two sides of the quadrangle were now formed.

Meanwhile, under Salvador Vallejo, work had begun on development of the Rancho Petaluma. Large sums of money were expended to establish a gigantic farming operation; vast acreage was placed under cultivation, and huge herds of cattle and sheep were introduced. The great, brooding, fortress-like house was begun in 1836, as the hub of the agricultural enterprise. Built of handmade adobe brick and roughhewn redwood timber, the two-story building formed an enormous quadrangle, about 200 feet square. The three-foot thick walls were plastered with mud and whitewashed with lime made from seashells. Sturdy wooden pegs secured the joists and

Two-storied barracks has rare cantilevered balcony.

The Petaluma Adobe

rafters, and handwrought hardware held together the lighter woodwork. Wide wooden balconies and an overhanging shingle roof protected the structure from damage by rain. Construction continued for more than a decade at a cost of $80,000.

The lower floor was devoted to warehouses and factories. Included were a large tannery that made shoes for the soldiers and vaqueros, and a blacksmith shop that produced spurs, tools, and other metal items. In another work area was a factory where wool was made into blankets, carpets, and cloth for wearing apparel. Upstairs were many large rooms, including a comfortable furnished apartment for the Vallejo family.

Each morning the workers assembled in the immense courtyard for roll call. Over 2000 Indians labored on the great rancho and were fed and clothed by its products. In 1843, the wheat and barley crop alone totaled better than 72,000 bushels, and a superabundance of other grains and vegetables was harvested. But mainstay of the ranch economy was the traffic in hides and tallow. Once a year in July, during the *matanza,* one fourth of the cattle herd was slaughtered, their hides becoming "banknotes" worth from fifteen to eighteen thousand dollars.

These were halcyon days for the Vallejos. *Comandante general* of the Northern Frontier, an area that today comprises nineteen counties, Don Mariano reigned supreme over his feudal principality. Then without warning, the powerful autocrat of Sonoma was arrested and made prisoner. A little before dawn on June 14, 1846, the *Casa Grande* was surrounded by a band of thirty-three Americans under the leadership of Ezekiel Merritt, Robert Semple, and William Ide, who demanded the surrender of the garrison and the town.

The dignified Don Mariano entertained the marauders with

Only half of the 200 ft. square quadrangle that
once formed General Vallejo's ranch residence
remains today.

Gentle wisteria drapes the balcony of the Blue Wing Inn.

food and drink while he quietly attempted to negotiate a peaceful settlement. After the Americans had agreed not to molest private property or his family, Vallejo gave them fifty horses and the keys to his storehouse. Still they insisted that he be taken as a captive to Sutter's Fort. These were the orders of John C. Frémont.

Also taken prisoner were Salvador Vallejo, Jacob Leese, and General Vallejo's secretary, Victor Prudon. Soon after their departure, Ide issued a flowery proclamation, declaring himself and his associates a republic. A flag was hastily fashioned out of white cloth, with a large lone star and a grizzly bear painted in pokeberry juice. The tri-colored banner of Mexico was lowered and the Bear Flag flew over the plaza of Sonoma.

Most of the Bear Flaggers were quartered in the barracks, next door to the *Casa Grande,* but some who sent for their families were housed in private adobes, including that of Salvador Vallejo on the northwest corner of the plaza. On the 9th of July, military representatives of the United States government arrived to raise the stars and stripes, and in August a company of the New York Volunteer Regiment occupied the barracks.

Meanwhile Mariano Vallejo was held prisoner for 48 days. So wearing was his ordeal that he weighed only 96 pounds when he returned from Sutter's Fort. At Sonoma he found that his Rancho Petaluma had been pillaged of over a thousand cattle and hundreds of horses. Still the great-hearted hidalgo harbored no grudges. Self-styled "foremost friend of the Americans", he supported the new government, lavished hospitality on visiting officials, and donated livestock to new settlers. Among those he befriended was Lilburn Boggs, future *alcalde* of Sonoma.

When the Boggs family arrived in the winter of 1846, after

Balcony supported by posts from ground to roof is most common in California adobes.

a grueling journey across the Sierra, Vallejo offered them the Petaluma adobe as a rent-free residence. Late at night, he rode forth to open the house, stringing lanterns on the upper balcony to guide the weary travelers. Rousing his Indian servants, he ordered supper prepared. Tables were spread with linen cloths, sperm candles were lighted in the chandeliers, and Don Mariano personally assisted in serving the sumptuous meal. Then he assigned a well-furnished apartment to the family and handed Mrs. Boggs the keys to the rest of the rooms.

The gold rush brought prosperity to Sonoma. It became the principal center of business north of San Francisco. Hotels and gambling saloons sprang up. One of these was the El Dorado Hotel in the old Vallejo adobe. Another was the Blue Wing Inn, operated by James Cooper and Thomas Spriggs. Located in an adobe structure opposite the ruins of the mission, the Inn was typical of the roaring forties—host to gamblers and miners with many a shoot-out within its walls. Incongruously, it

Ray-Adler adobe, a short block from the mission.

was also a family operation, with Cooper's young sons working as waiters. Exuberant miners tossed gold nuggets into the boys' aprons and the lucky chaps garnered additional treasure simply by sweeping the gold dust off the barroom floor.

For several years, Sonoma was also the focal point of military affairs. Headquarters of the army's Pacific Division was in the old Leese adobe, and troops of the United States Dragoons were based in the barracks. But by 1852, the military withdrew, much of the gold bonanza was over, and relative quiet settled over the town. Still, the plaza could be a hectic place, with bronco-busting contests, dog and coon fights, and horse racing.

In 1854, the Vallejo family moved into their new Victorian mansion at Lachryma Montis, and the *Casa Grande* was rented as a school. Despite the luxury of their residence, the fortunes of the family were waning. Legal costs for defending title to holdings before the United States Land Commission and the higher courts had placed Don Mariano in severe financial difficulties. He was forced to lease portions of the Rancho Petaluma, which had never recovered its productivity after the Mexican-American War. Slowly the magnificent Petaluma adobe began to deteriorate. In 1857, Vallejo sold the great house and adjoining land for $25,000. The once proud building, the symbol of Vallejo's triumph over the frontier, continued to crumble.

Then, in 1867, a second symbol was swept away, as fire demolished the *Casa Grande.* Only the servants' quarters and some scarred adobe walls remained. Soon other structures occupied the site. Sonoma was changing. It no longer belonged to the Lord of the North.

Today a number of old adobes still stand in the old pueblo. They are in various stages of preservation and restoration. On the plaza are the Leese house and the two Salvador Vallejo adobes, all in commercial use. The servants' quarters of the *Casa Grande* and the barracks belong to the state and are in the process of restoration. Around the corner is the Blue Wing Inn, privately owned and in good condition, and across from it is the reconstructed mission. There are also several private adobes along the side streets. But for the feeling and flavor of Vallejo's Sonoma, one must make a pilgrimage out of town.

Eleven miles west of Sonoma, high on a hilltop overlooking a wide vista of rolling, oak-studded hills, stands the Petaluma adobe, miraculously restored. Acquired by the Native Sons of the Golden West in 1910, it was deeded to the state in 1951. Half of the great quadrangle was saved and beautifully reconstructed. Furnished to recreate its period, the house now stands as a completely unique representation of California rancho days. To visit it is indeed an awe-inspiring experience.

One of Monterey's oldest adobes.

Casa de Soto

The Sotos were sturdy Monterey pioneers, descended from members of the de Anza expedition. In 1823, José Joaquín Soto, then a youth of twenty, married María del Carmen Castro and, for his bride, built a three-room adobe atop a knoll overlooking Monterey Bay, above present-day Eldorado Street, on land which he had purchased from relatives. The little rectangular house was fashioned of handmade adobe bricks, plastered with a mixture of mud and twigs, and roofed with tule. Small openings served as windows. Near the doorstep, he built a bake oven for cooking. This dwelling, the Casa de Soto, was to be home to four generations of Sotos over a period of almost a hundred years.

Joaquín and María had nine children. To provide for his large family, Joaquín petitioned for acreage on which he could raise stock and cultivate crops, and in 1842 he was granted the Rancho El Piojo, on the Nacimiento River in the Santa Lucia Mountains. To meet the conditions of the grant, he not only occupied the land with cattle and sheep but also built a house upon it where he resided for portions of the year while farming about 200 acres of the 13,330-acre tract.

Seven years after Joaquín's death, in 1852, his widow was forced to sell the Rancho El Piojo for the payment of debts and the support of her family. It was the beginning of a series of Soto family misfortunes which eventually found María and Joaquín's grandson, Augustin, practically penniless and living with his numerous children in a tumbledown shack built in front of the old adobe—which was by then falling apart and uninhabitable. Affectionately known among the townspeople as "old Count Soto," Augustin was said to have reflected in his demeanor dignity and old world charm. In 1938, when he was in his seventies, the Soto's long occupancy of the property was brought to an end. Unpaid taxes and the unkempt condition of the place resulted in eviction of the family by the city. The shanty was torn down and the adobe left to disintegrate. Half-hidden by weeds, with boarded-over windows and an age-blackened tile roof, it stood for several years as a forlorn relic of the past.

Meanwhile, Mary Greene, a woman with a will, struggled with a mass of legal detail in an attempt to purchase the property. Curator of the Custom House, Mrs. Green was determined to preserve the venerable adobe as a rare example of the simple kind of dwelling built in the area at the beginning of the nineteenth century. Finally, in 1945, she was able to obtain clear title and make the little house her own. She then spent six years on its restoration, adding a bedroom wing but making sure that the essential character of the building was not altered. Though not herself a Catholic, she even followed the old Spanish tradition of having the adobe blessed before she took up residence in it. She lived in her beloved *casa* until 1958, when she left the community and sold it to a physician. The building, now used for medical offices, still possesses much of its power to conjure the aura of bygone days.

Mellow afternoon sunlight illuminates
Stevenson house bedroom.

The Stevenson House

For maybe a month, in 1879, Robert Louis Stevenson occupied a room in the adobe building in Monterey which now bears his name. But in addition to its brief association with the famous author, the house on Houston Street has a fascinating history of its own. The original, two-story adobe is now all but obscured by the many changes the building has undergone in a multitude of commercial uses. Built in 1841 by José Rafael Gonzales, the house comprised what is today the grand *sala* and one large upstairs room. This portion of the building stood on the back of the lot and possibly had its entrance toward present-day Tyler Street.

Lieutenant Gonzalez came to Monterey with the newly appointed Governor Figueroa in 1833 and held several important government positions, including that of *alcalde.* Then, for a time he lived in San Juan Bautista, returning to the capital in 1841 when he was granted a large town lot behind the newly constructed government offices, *El Cuartel.* On it he dreamed of erecting a "little castle" modeled after a grand *casa* in his home town in Mexico. He settled, however, for simpler architecture and actually lived in the house only intermittently.

In January of 1856, perhaps to raise funds for litigation involving his land grants, Gonzalez sold the house and surrounding property to José Abrego, who, a month later, resold it to Jean Girardin, a native of Switzerland, and his business partner, Pablo Fassanini. Several small adobes now stood on the lot, but for the comfortable accommodation of his wife

Houston street facade as constructed by Jean Girardin.

Metate y mano in left foreground typifies the most-used kitchen implement in early California.

Deep-reveal window and 2" redwood planking are details in original *sala*.

and children, Girardin added a sizeable section to the main building on the Houston Street side. The family residence was on the upper floor and consisted of a parlor and three bedrooms, one of which is now displayed as "the children's room." The rest of the building was rented out for a number of business enterprises.

In later years, the large center room beneath the Girardin apartment was for a time a tavern run by Girardin's son-in-law and, after that, a carriage shop. Above the *sala,* in the original adobe, Girardin maintained a billiard room. After Girardin's death, in 1879, his widow rented rooms in the building, and it came to be called the French Hotel. It was then, in the fall of that year, that Stevenson resided there very briefly. For some time, the artist Jules Tavernier had his studio in the room across the hall from the Girardin's parlor.

Gradually, the building deteriorated and became a haven for poor families. Then, after the turn of the century, it became a boardinghouse and artists' rendezvous, with the former billiard room partitioned into small bedroom cubicles. Parties were held in the walled-in garden and on the beautiful, broad-planked, redwood floor in the *sala,* where a colorful bohemian crowd danced away the hours. In the 1930s, the artist August Gay occupied what had been the Tavernier studio as well as part of the old Girardin apartment, and the noted decorator, Frances Elkins, had a workshop downstairs. Finally, in 1937, when there was a threat that the old building might be torn down, it was purchased by Edith C. van Antwerp and Mrs. C. Tobin Clark. They saved it from destruction and, in 1942, gave it to the State of California. Carefully renovated, it is now a museum and houses a fine collection of Stevensoniana.

Small rear balcony gave access to the rooms of Jules Tavernier, the artist, and Robert Louis Stevenson, the writer.

Under three family ownerships, Stokes, Escolle, and Gragg, this gracious house was always a center of hospitality.

The Stokes Adobe

For more than a century, the building that stands astride present-day Hartnell and Polk Streets in Monterey was the scene of abundant family life. When James Stokes purchased the tile-roofed adobe, in 1837, it consisted of one room with a partition separating the bedroom. Three years later, Stokes married Joséfa Soto de Cano, a widow with four children, and soon the couple had offspring of their own. The tiny dwelling could not accommodate the burgeoning brood, so it was gradually enlarged until, in 1848, it had become a two-story house with seven rooms and a wing for the kitchen and storeroom. Inside the stone walls that surrounded the property were additional wooden sheds, one of which housed for a time the press that produced California's first newspaper, the *Californian.* Stokes was a man of many occupations, acting as physician and druggist to the citizens of Monterey as well as maintaining a general store in his home, which came to be called the *"Gran Barata,"* meaning "big bargain."

The tranquility of the Stokes' menage is reflected in a scene recorded by Walter Colton, at one time the *alcalde* of Monterey and a frequent guest of the hospitable Stokes family:

"It was evening, and the hour for rest . . . when six little boys and girls knelt around the chair of their father, repeating the Lord's prayer, and closing with . . . God bless our dear parents. What are the gold mines to this? A glow-worm's light beneath a star that shall never set!"

The star was extinguished in 1855, with the death of Doña Joséfa. By then, Stokes was a man of property, with large holdings in San Jose as well as Monterey County. But a second marriage to a Southern belle did not bring him happiness and, in 1864, James Stokes ended his life by suicide.

Executors of the Stokes estate sold the Monterey adobe to Honore Escolle, a successful French merchant in Monterey, for $2,000 in gold. Occupying the house with his large family, Escolle once again brought laughter and the sound of children's voices to its spacious rooms. He also brought a new enterprise to the property when he decided to experiment with using the clay to make pottery. Back of his house he built a small kiln, which is still standing, and soon he was manufacturing flower pots and tiles that found a ready market in San Francisco. Eventually the owner of much of the land on which the town of Carmel is now situated, Escolle also became a prosperous orchardist and dairy farmer, with huge acreage in three counties. Though the Escolles spent their summers in a splendid country residence in the Salinas Valley, the Stokes adobe in Monterey remained their home until the late 1890s.

After the turn of the century, the property was acquired by Mortimer and Martha Harriet Gragg. Prominent in the social life of Monterey, the beautiful, blonde Hattie Gragg made her home a center of festivity until her death in 1948. A restaurant of considerable renown now occupies the premises.

The José Remigio de la Torre adobe.

The de la Torre Adobes

Two of old Monterey's charming, smaller adobes are still standing a short distance apart, one on the corner of present-day Polk and Hartnell Streets and the other near Colton Hall at Jefferson and Pierce Streets. Each was owned by a son of José Joaquín de la Torre, a pioneer Spanish soldier who had come to Monterey in 1801. Gabriel, de la Torre's second oldest son, was capable and courageous and had advanced rapidly in his military career when, in 1841, he was granted a town lot in Monterey, across from the Stokes adobe. On the lot he built a three-room house, and there he dwelt with his second wife Juana and the children of both his marriages. For over fifty years, the adobe remained the family home of the de la Torres. The claim that it was also the site of the first federal court is somewhat ambiguous. Possibly it rests on the fact that Gabriel, who was justice of the peace during the 1850s, may have rented a room in the house to the federal district commissioner for use as a courtroom.

Juana de la Torre, who outlived her husband by about twenty years, became famous as a *partera* (midwife). Women journeyed from far up the Salinas Valley to have their babies in the home of the highly skilled old lady, and it was there that Robert Johnson, a future mayor of Monterey, was born. After Juana's death the house was sold and, early in the 1900s, it was transformed into a tea room.

For about forty years, the tea room, combined after a time with a gift and book shop, was eminently successful. A two-

Small wooden addition complements original adobe.

Large north window added recently for benefit of artist-owner.

story wing was added to the old adobe, where delicious cakes were baked and tea was served in the small patio garden amidst the ancient flowering fruit trees. After 1946, the business in the de la Torre adobe was confined to a bookstore, and finally, in 1958, the property was purchased for the offices of a prominent law firm. Still carefully preserved, the adobe is a fine example of conservation combined with use.

The second de la Torre adobe, on the southwest corner of Jefferson and Pierce Streets, belonged to Gabriel's younger brother, José Remigio. Born in 1831, José Remigio lived for many years in the Big Sur area, south of the Post property. Then, in 1862, he purchased the three-room Monterey adobe which Francisco Pinto had built some ten years earlier. The *casa* remained in possession of the family for over half a century, being home to José Remigio's married daughter María, and then to her children.

In 1924, the adobe was purchased by the Myron Olivers, who owned it for thirty years. An artist and craftsman, Mr. Oliver was a leader in the movement to preserve Monterey's architectural heritage. Though several frame structures have been added to the adobe and a large window opened in the north wall, its charm is intact. Today, still privately owned, the dwelling represents an interesting adaptation of adobe construction to contemporary life style.

The Gabriel de la Torre adobe.

The Trescony Adobes

High west wall of the one hundred year old adobe barn.

East of the great wall of the Santa Lucia Mountains, in the southern portion of the Salinas Valley, lies the Rancho San Lucas. There, cupped in undulating, oak-studded hills, are six century-old adobes. Built by Alberto Trescony, in the 1860s, they are still the center of a huge working ranch and homestead to three generations of his descendants.

Born in Italy, Trescony was orphaned at an early age. When he was twelve, he ran away from home to Paris, where he learned to be a tinsmith. About fourteen years later, he emigrated to the United States and worked his way across the country from New York to Texas. He saved enough money to buy a small herd of sheep, which he drove to Mexico and sold for a good price. Then by walking from Mexico City to Mazatlan to conserve his capital, he was able to book a steamer bound for California. He landed at Monterey in 1842.

Living in a shack, the frugal Italian worked at his trade of tinsmith. Suddenly, with the advent of the gold rush, tin pans were selling to prospectors at $35 each and his business flourished. Within a few years, he amassed a fortune of $50,000 and became the owner of several hotels. But he was not content to be an innkeeper. He also began buying sheep, which at first he pastured on rented acreage. Then came the opportunity to acquire land of his own: the Rancho San Lucas, 8875 acres of deeply carpeted grassland that had once been the grant of the Estrada family, was for sale for $3,000. In 1862, the rancho became the property of Trescony.

Six century-old adobes are clustered in this fertile valley.

Built by Alberto Trescony, this has been home for four generations of the family.

their holdings and renting out land to tenant farmers. Then the astute Julius gave the railroad a right-of-way through the vast Trescony property and laid out a town around the projected railway station. By 1890, the town of San Lucas had become the principal shipping and supply station for the southern section of the Salinas Valley.

While Alberto Trescony's vision of a giant agricultural enterprise was being brought to fruition by his son, the old gentleman dreamed away the hours—thinking of how an Italian tinsmith had become one of the largest landowners in Monterey County. In 1892, he died at the age of eighty and was buried on a knoll at a point overlooking his three ranchos. An elaborate memorial statue was placed at the grave, visible from present-day highway 101.

Today, the Trescony adobes are in immaculate condition, and all continue to be used for functional purposes. The magnificent barn, which has the appearance of a two-story building, still has its original flooring intact. The adobe house, though equipped with modern appurtenances, is essentially unchanged. In it resides Alberto Trescony's grandson, Julius II, and his children and grandchildren. For the Tresconys, the heritage of early California lives on.

Bunkhouse was constructed to house farmhands when ranch was expanded in 1870s.

The José de Jesús Vallejo Adobe

In the Niles District of Fremont stands a rare example of the life-style of early California: a lovely one-room adobe amidst the gardens of the California Nursery Company. Built by José de Jesús Vallejo immediately after he received the 17,705-acre Rancho Arroyo de la Alameda in 1842, the small structure satisfied the requirement that a house be erected within a year after a grant was given.

Born in the pueblo of San Jose, in 1798, Don José was the second son of Ignacio Vicente Ferrer Vallejo and an older brother of General Mariano Vallejo. As a young man, José lived on his father's rancho in the Monterey area, then moved to Mission San Jose in 1836, when he was appointed its administrator. Five years later he became military *comandante* of the town. Deciding to spend the rest of his life in the place of his birth, he petitioned for land in the beautiful, fertile valley to the north. The little adobe, first of several he constructed on his vast acreage, was occupied by the *mayordomo,* or overseer of his ranch employees.

By the 1850s, huge herds of cattle roamed the rancho and two flour mills had been built in the valley of the Alameda. Don José, his wife, and their daughters, now resided in an elegant, 18-room house across from the San Jose mission. Vallejo had achieved a position of prestige and affluence in the community. But then, like locusts, disappointed and destitute argonauts descended on his lands, and much of Don José's wealth was drained away by law suits he brought to drive out the squatters, who numbered as many as 600 at one time. But he managed to hold on to his property, at least for another couple of decades.

The original adobe remained primitive. In the 1860s it was occupied by one of Vallejo's workers—a Portuguese *vaquero* and his wife and children. At that time it still had a dirt floor, one door, and only a hole in the tile roof for ventilation. The rectangular room was divided into four areas—one for sleeping, one close to the fireplace for cooking, one for the household animals, and one where an altar stood for daily

This one room adobe was built by José de Jesús Vallejo, brother of the general, to satisfy requirements that a house be built within a year after a grant was given.

prayers. Despite their cramped quarters, the family was expected to take in occasional travelers and put them up for the night!

In 1884, the California Nursery Company purchased 600 acres of the Rancho Arroyo de la Alameda and moved their nursery operation there from San Jose. Some thirty years later George Roeding acquired the property, and in the early 1930s, his son decided to restore the old adobe on the nursery grounds. Used by the Roedings as a guest house and for public celebrations, the building has been carefully refurbished but little altered. Though the floor is now tile and several deep-embrasured windows bring in the sunlight, the heavy exposed beams and tile roof are unchanged. Great charm radiates from the ancient walls. Simple and unadorned, the adobe stands as a beautiful evocation of a little-known aspect of early California living.

Under cantilevered balcony is the only remnant
of Monterey's early whalebone sidewalk.

The Whaling Station

Best known now as a former boardinghouse for whalers, the two-story adobe called the Whaling Station was built by an Englishman, David Wight, as a replica of his family's ancestral cottage in Scotland. Wight had sailed for California with his wife and daughter in the mid-1840s. Arriving in Monterey shortly after the American occupation, he purchased a piece of land and, with the help of his neighbor, Gallant Dickenson, constructed his dwelling after the design he remembered—low-ceilinged rooms opening into a narrow hall and a central stairway. His one substitution was adobe for stone.

A short time later, Wight succumbed to gold fever and left Monterey for the mines in 1849. He got a good price for his adobe, however, selling it to Alberto Trescony for $5,500. The Italian tinsmith Trescony, who already owned the Washington Hotel in Monterey, turned the Wight adobe into another roominghouse. A few years later, in 1855, when a group of Portuguese whalers organized a company for the purpose of shore-whaling in Monterey Bay, Trescony leased his new property to them as their headquarters.

For a couple of decades the Portuguese group, which became known as the "Old Company," carried on a lucrative business, taking as much as 1,700 barrels of oil in a season. The company's rendering works was on the beach directly to the north of the building. At the center of the works was a crude shack comprising a washroom, drying room, and cooper's shop. Outside were huge vats of planking which held the

The oak and the anchor are reminiscent of Monterey's past.

blubber as it was stripped from the carcass. And next to these were enormous kettles, set in a rude furnace formed of rocks and clay, in which the whale fat was rendered into oil. Thick black clouds of smoke, the stench overpowering, rose from the steaming pots.

In 1864, Captain Joseph Pray, commander of the "Old Company," purchased the adobe—known by then as the Whaling Station—from Mr. Trescony for $500. This was less than a tenth of what Trescony had paid for it some fifteen years earlier. The startling devaluation of the property is indicative of the severe depression which engulfed Monterey soon after the middle of the 1850s.

Over the years the Whaling Station was preserved by successive tenants, one of whom added the graceful balcony. Today, the adobe, with the ancient whalebone sidewalk along its front and the beautiful gardens surrounded by a high chalk-rock wall remains redolent of the charm of old Monterey.

Quiet, sheltered garden in the midst of downtown Monterey recreates an earlier tranquility.

Photo Notes

All photographs except the interiors of Larkin and Stevenson houses, Casa Amesti, and the Customs House were made with an 8x10 Ansco view camera. On it, the following lenses were used:

19" Goerz Artar
15" Zeiss Apo-Tessar
12" Goerz Dagor
10" Goerz Dagor
8¼" Schneider Symar
6¼" Cooke Anastigmat
121 mm. Schneider Super-Angulon.

Wherever possible, exteriors were made with the 19" Artar, a lens with which, granting ample space, I invariably work. It is not misleading to say that I always reach for the longest lens commensurate with the way in which I wish material to be seen. If I have a favorite, the 19" must be it. More often than not, regardless of its special characteristics as a lens, I "see" this way.

If a view through a long lens with its detached perspective lacks vitality or interest, I readily go to a shorter one. For architectural purposes, I wish many times to give more drawing power to dominant lines, and to do so, often requires shorter rather than longer lenses.

To be sure, the use of short lenses tends to draw attention to lineal values, especially when they run to or from the camera. But contrary to what I often hear about short lenses, the use of perspective depends not on the lens but on the photographer.

(Short and long here refer to focal length of a lens. When focal length is less than the diagonal of a given film size, the lens is called short: as an 8¼" lens on 8x10 film, a 5¼" lens on 4x5 film, and a 35mm. on 35mm film. Conversely, a long lens is a 19" on 8x10, a 10" on 4x5, or a 90mm. on 35 mm. film.)

Reproduction often obscures the true value of a lens, but a few characteristics of the lenses I use may be worth pointing out in relation to photographic print quality. The Artar, Symar, and Super-Angulon lenses give me the most brilliant negatives with hardly any ascertainable differences, except of course those of perspective. Each "eats into the shadows" equally well and records high values with a crystalline subtlety that I have come to believe is what I "see" in any given photograph.

The Cooke Anastigmat is unusual, but of another breed. It does not produce the same brilliance which I have come to expect from the trio. Closed down to f32 or f45, it has a clean resolution which stands up well under my scrutiny through an eight or ten-power glass. At wider stops, it gives a "softness" or "rounded quality" to material of which in photographing architecture I rarely take advantage, and which has nothing to do with fuzziness. Despite these other than looked-for characteristics, I have used the Cooke now with delight for about twenty years and have steadfastly resisted the opportunity to be consistent and to exchange it for a Super-Angulon or Symar of about the same focal length.

And this brings us to covering power, also of great importance when photographing buildings with a view camera, and in close quarters. The short lenses have their various built-in limits which I am always trying to stretch on the flexibility of the large view camera. The Cooke has the greatest relative covering power, the Dagors are more than acceptable, and the Symar is a downright nuisance. Its close limits often make me move closer to a subject and put the Cooke in its place. The Super-Angulon, rarely used on 8x10 in such a short focal length, allows no lens movement at all when working at infinity. In fact, it vignettes slightly. But in extreme situations, the Super-Angulon has proven invaluable even without adequate covering power.

Eastman's Super XX and Agfapan 200 have been my standard films in the 8x10 size for some years. After careful metering, and imposing my own judgment on what the meter tells me, I expose either film at ASA:160 for development in a Pyro solution, also of long familiarity. I find Pyro's soft quality and latitude generally more pleasing than any of the more precise modern developers, at least for what and how I see. A slight alteration of Pyro components provides the same normal development for either film. Super XX always gives a slightly better compression of brightness values, as Agfapan 200 produces a better expansion. The differences are so slight, I have long used the films interchangeably.

On many subjects of contemporary architectural interest, I produce a set of prints which are the result of working with both the large view camera and the smaller Hasselblad. Prints in 8x10 from 2¼" negatives compare favorably, at least to my eye, with the same size prints made from 8x10 negatives if, *with great care,* both size negatives have gone through the same or similar optics for printing. One's conception and sense of quality must occasionally over-ride other considerations.

The use of two cameras of such different characteristics seems in no way inconsistent if high standards of purpose and method are maintained. No doubt I "see" and "feel" much better with the 8x10 view camera in hand. It is as if I played the piano for many years and felt more at home with it than with other instruments, but occasionally went to the flute or the oboe for different sounds. So, as a photographer at one with a chosen camera, I alter "dimension" and "feeling" by using on occasion another camera, or for that matter, different lenses, films, filters, etc.

So I like to "see" with the particular characteristics of camera and lens well in mind. But I find that photographs are stamped by many factors, by an accumulation of many elements, certainly not by camera and lens alone. Film and film developers, paper and paper developers have a decided bearing. The ways each are used become even greater determinants within the equation. Ultimately, individualism in photography as in other expressive fields, depends far more on personal proclivities and a familiar experience in the force of expressing them than on equipment, materials, and methods.